The Spokesman

Full Spectrum Absurdity
Will America Die of Defence?

Edited by Ken Coates

Published by Spokesman for the
Bertrand Russell Peace Foundation

Spokesman 71   2001

CONTENTS

Editorial	3	
The Current Crises in the Middle East	9	*Noam Chomsky*
Nuclear Warfare Revisited	30	*Ken Coates*
The Militarist Camp in the United States	42	*Immanuel Wallerstein*
Missile Defence: Pretext Absurd	45	*Joseph Rotblat*
Satellite Killers and Space Dominance	47	*Bob Aldridge*
Scapegoats ands Feral Cats	56	*John Kinsella*
Stop the Ilisu Dam	60	*Martin Hall*
Keynes: Man of Peace	64	*Michael Barratt Brown*
Peace Dossier	71	
Reviews	81	*Michael Barratt Brown* *Ken Coates* *James Smith* *Pamela White*

Printed by the Russell Press Ltd., Nottingham, UK

ISSN 0262 7922   ISBN 0 85124 647 8

Subscriptions
Institutions £30.00
Individuals £20.00

Back issues available on request

A CIP catalogue record for this book is available from the British Library

Published by the
Bertrand Russell Peace Foundation Ltd.,
Russell House
Bulwell Lane
Nottingham NG6 0BT
England
Tel. 0115 9784504
email:
elfeuro@compuserve.com
www.spokesmanbooks.com
www.russfound.org

Editorial Board:
Michael Barratt Brown
Ken Coates
John Daniels
Ken Fleet
Stuart Holland
Tony Simpson

Minority Rights Group International

'critical information unavailable elsewhere'

Minority Rights Group International (MRG) is a non-governmental organization (NGO) working to secure rights for ethnic, religious and linguistic minorities worldwide, and to promote cooperation and understanding between communities.

MRG has over 30 years experience of promoting the rights of marginalized, indigenous and non-dominant groups within society. It does this by researching and publishing on minority rights issues, and seeking to raise awareness through its advocacy and outreach among governments and international institutions, NGOs, activists, the media, the general public and minority groups. MRG aims to promote the importance of minority rights and to promote an awareness of the international laws, conventions and procedures that exist to protect them.

Due to its contacts with minority groups, NGO's, governments and international bodies, MRG is in a unique position to ensure that this awareness-raising on minority rights, results in the development of practical policies and programmes which have positive and direct impact, thereby promoting minority rights and conflict prevention.

To find out more about Minority Rights Group, order our free publications catalogue or subscribe to our reports, please contact us quoting ref: SPK or visit our website.

UK Office:
Tel: +44 (0)20 7978 9498
Fax: +44 (0)20 7738 6265
E-mail: minority.rights@mrgmail.org
379 Brixton Road, London, SW9 7DE, UK.

MRG Publications

World Directory of Minorities:
MRG's 856 page reference book covering over 700 minority groups in more than 200 states and dependent territories.

Reports:
Recent titles include:
The Palestinians, Muslim Women in India, Cyprus, Eritrea, Central Asia, Minority Rights in Yugoslavia, Refugees in Europe and The Kurds.

Books:
Titles include:
Cutting the Rose - Female Genital Mutilation, The Palestinians, Polar Peoples, and Scorpians in a Bottle: Conflicting cultures in Northern Ireland.

Educational Publications:
Titles include:
Voices from Sudan, Angola, Uganda, Eritrea, Somalia and Kurdistan; Forging New Identities.

www.minorityrights.org

Editorial

'The ultimate goal of our military force is to accomplish the objectives directed by the National Command Authorities. For the joint force of the future, this goal will be achieved through full spectrum dominance – the ability of US forces, operating unilaterally or in combination with multinational and interagency partners, to defeat any adversary and control any situation across the full range of military operations.

The full range of operations includes maintaining a posture of strategic deterrence. It includes theater engagement and presence activities. It includes conflict involving employment of strategic forces and weapons of mass destruction, major theater wars, regional conflicts, and smaller-scale contingencies. It also includes those ambiguous situations residing between peace and war, such as peacekeeping and peace enforcement operations, as well as noncombat humanitarian relief operations and support to domestic authorities.

The label full spectrum dominance implies that US forces are able to conduct prompt, sustained, and synchronized operations with combinations of forces tailored to specific situations and with access to and freedom to operate in all domains – space, sea, land, air, and information. Additionally, given the global nature of our interests and obligations, the United States must maintain its overseas presence forces and the ability to rapidly project power worldwide in order to achieve full spectrum dominance.'

United States Department of Defence: ***Joint Vision 2020****, 30th May 2000*

For many years students of military doctrine have needed some lifeline, to maintain an ever more tenuous link with reality. The explosion of technical capacity has blown apart old notions of what constitutes reality. If this mental upheaval had liberated men's imaginations to engage such problems as world poverty, there might have been much good in it. But such concerns are not respectable among practical statesmen, who find it easier to look into the problems of domination.

'Full spectrum dominance' is a product of prolonged thinking of the unthinkable, and it is a permanent preoccupation of some of the more thoughtful members of the military establishment of the United States. Those whom the Gods would destroy …

Now the Western press reports that within weeks of his installation, President Bush is already planning to withdraw from the Anti-Ballistic Missile Treaty of 1972, widely seen as a pillar of global security. For Secretary of Defence Donald Rumsfeld, this Treaty is reported to be 'ancient history', and by an Orwellian leap, 'Cold War thinking'. That is why Senator Jon Kyl, a member of the Intelligence Committee, can insist that the administration is 'poised to withdraw'. For him, the Treaty is 'an anachronism of the Cold War that prevents us dealing effectively with the threats of the 21st century'.

And these threats are? In all seriousness, John Barry has informed the readers of **Prospect** that Rumsfeld's fears were validated on the 31st August 1998 by the launch of a North Korean missile, the Taepo Dong-1, which 'turned out to have a third stage'. If it had worked, this third stage would have given the missile an intercontinental range. But this pig did not fly: it fell in the sea.

Other pigs cannot fly, either. The missile which the North Korean leaders would have liked to have had matches the National Missile Defence which President Bush would also like to have. Somebody has drawn a good picture of the idea: but up to now nobody has found out how to make it work. Billions of dollars have been lavished on NMD, and billions more are earmarked. But imaginary NMD, so far, equals imaginary Taepo Dong. The seas are full of the by products of this military imagination.

Would it not be possible just to imagine other expensive systems, without actually spending all that money on them? But the logic of full spectrum dominance does not work in such a way. Let John Barry explain:

> 'If North Korea – bankrupt, primitive, starving, isolated North Korea – could develop something close to an Inter-Continental Ballistic Missile (ICBM), the world really was a more threatening place.'

The logical conclusion was, he went on,

> 'America's thirty-five year debate about missile defences was suddenly over'.

For those who retain that subversive link with reality, of course, the argument is that because North Korea can draw a picture of a three-stage missile, America should draw more pictures of an anti-missile shield. After spending obscene amounts of money, both countries can initiate tests, neither of which may function. But the real world is really mad, and the mere thought that if those poverty stricken Koreans tried hard, they might one day find a way of getting their third stage to work, implies that full spectrum dominance depends on an American capacity to shoot it down, even if it is down already.

To this end, the allies must be intimidated into believing that deployment is inevitable. The adversaries, (yesterday's 'partners', and today's 'competitors',) must also be intimidated. But they have a choice. They can, if they do not approve of the unilateral destruction of the ABM Treaty, manufacture very large numbers of missiles capable of saturating the new defence, even before it has been finally perfected. As President Chirac has informed us

> 'This is the age-old battle between the sword and the shield: and invariably the sword will win.'

President Bush has lost no time whatever in asserting the practical consequences of full spectrum dominance. Unfortunately, he has enunciated the consequences of the new doctrine before he has set its material prerequisites in place.

In the year 2000, President Jiang Zemin of China, and Russian President Putin issued a joint statement to insist that it is 'of vital importance to maintain and strictly observe the ABM Treaty'. Both China and Russia have the means, if not the wish, to multiply their strategic nuclear arsenals to the point which could swamp the new defence of the United States, if we were to accept that an early and workable prototype of National Missile Defence could actually be set in place. In spite of the fact that President Bush has not yet achieved his aim, his frequent insistence on it has caused alarm in chancelleries all around the world, and could indeed provoke the very proliferation of nukes which he aims to inhibit.

To enforce respect for his dominance, President Bush has also unilaterally withdrawn from the Kyoto agreements to control global warming, and has provoked very general hostility among all those States which laboured to refine an agreement on global warming. As if to emphasise the issues at stake, an American spy plane is grounded on Hainan Island, and the United States and China are locked in an intricate disputation about whether President Bush knows how to apologise for spying on his 'competitor'. Is all this so far removed from the dogma of full spectrum dominance? Nobody thinks that Chinese planes have a right to cruise the American seaboard, in order to pick up titbits of electronic information, or messages from nuclear submarines. Is it not, after all, an American century, and an American globe?

Pride comes before a fall. Roy Medvedev has shown, in his percipient study of Russian history since the end of the Soviet Union, how much responsibility for the crisis of the Russian economy should be laid at the door of the military industrial complex. To stay abreast in the production of rockets, nuclear submarines, and aircraft carriers, Russia ruined itself. More and more of the cleverest people were deployed in military production, and more and more investment was swallowed up by it. Unkind critics called the Soviet Union Upper Volta with rockets. But the rockets did not maintain the integrity of the Soviet Union: they rather contributed to its disintegration.

Could the pursuit of full spectrum dominance lead into the achievement of its opposite? The American economy is phenomenally productive, and it seems unthinkable that it should falter, no matter how many mad projects are foisted on it. But the mentality of dominance is the secret weapon of self-destruction. Maybe the inauguration of President Bush began something quite novel: the long haul to the re-education of America, and the reduction of domination to absurdity.

Ken Coates

The Botany Case
The Rise and Fall of Full Spectrum Dominance

Sir Brian had a battle-axe with great big knobs on.
He went among the villagers and blipped them on the head.
On Wednesday and on Saturday,
Especially on the latter day,
He called on all the cottages and this is what he said:

"I am Sir Brian!" (Ting-ling!)
"I am Sir Brian!" (Rat-tat!)
"I am Sir Brian,
"As bold as a lion!
"Take that, and that, and that!"

Sir Brian had a pair of boots with great big spurs on;.
A fighting pair of which he was particularly fond.
On Tuesday and on Friday,
Just to make the street look tidy,
He'd collect the passing villagers and kick them in the pond.

"I am Sir Brian!" (Sper-lash!)
"I am Sir Brian!" (Sper-losh!)
"I am Sir Brian,
"As bold as a Lion!
"Is anyone else for a wash?"

Sir Brian woke one morning and he couldn't find his battle-axe.
He walked into the village in his second pair of boots.
He had gone a hundred paces
When the street was full of faces
And the villagers were 'round him with ironical salutes.

"You are Sir Brian? My, my.
"You are Sir Brian? Dear, dear.
"You are Sir Brian
"As bold as a lion?
"Delighted to meet you here!"

Sir Brian went a journey and he found a lot of duckweed.
They pulled him out and dried him and they blipped him on the head.
They took him by the breeches
And they hurled him into ditches
And they pushed him under waterfalls and this is what they said:

"You are Sir Brian — don't laugh!
"You are Sir Brian — don't cry!
"You are Sir Brian
"As bold as a lion —
"Sir Brian the Lion, goodbye!"

Sir Brian struggled home again and chopped up his battle-axe.
Sir Brian took his fighting boots and threw them in the fire.
He is quite a different person
Now he hasn't got his spurs on,
And he goes about the village as B. Botany, Esquire.

"I am Sir Brian? Oh, no!
"I am Sir Brian? Who's he?
"I haven't any title, I'm Botany;
"Plain Mr. Botany (B.)"

by A.A.Milne

NEW LEFT REVIEW

6 NOV/DEC 2000

Robin Blackburn *Cuba on the Block*
David Harvey *Reinventing Geography*
Michael Maar *Deadly Potions*
Fredric Jameson *Taking on Globalization*
Yang Lian *Back to Beijing*
Franco Moretti
Ross McKibbin
Joel Handler
Daniele Archibugi

5 SEP/OCT 2000

Tariq Ali *Throttling Iraq*
Asada Akira *The Place of Nothingness*
Sabry Hafez *Banquet for Seaweed*
He Qinglian *China's Listing Mansion*
J. G. A. Pocock *Gaberlunzie's Return*

4 JULY/AUG 2000

Robert Brenner *The Boom and the Bubble*
Edward Said *America's Last Taboo*
Wang Hui *A New Left in China*
Peter Wollen *Derek Jarman's Blue*
Ronald Dore *Worldwide Anglo-Saxonism?*
...ial Justice'
...ge of Convergence

8 MAR/APR 2001

Brian Barry *Multicultural Muddles*
John Grahl *Globalized Finance*
Bertell Ollman *The Emperor and the Yakuza*
Hal Foster *Art Criticism, R. I. P.?*
Peter Wollen *A Psychogeography of Chance*
Perry Anderson *Testing Formula Two*

Peter Gowan
Origins of Atlantic Liberalism

Christopher Prendergast
Casanova's Literary Cosmos

7 JAN/FEB 2001

Jorge Castañeda *Mexico on the Turn*
Jack Goody *Bitter Icons*
Stefan Collini *Mulhern's 'Metaculture'*
Tom Nairn *Post-Ukania*
Michael Maar *In Bluebeard's Chamber*
Timothy Brennan *Rooted Cosmopolitanism*
David Ladipo *Imprisoned America*
Robert Wade *Culling the World Bank*
Tony Wood *Aleksei German*

Gavan McCormack
Japan's Houdini

...mes King
of Clintonomics
...he Anti-Nietzsche?

Franco Moretti *World Literature*
Taggart Murphy *Japan's Economic Crisis*
Tom Nairn *Blair's Ukania*
Peter Wollen *Magritte and the Bowler Hat*
Perry Anderson *Renewals*

Benedict Anderson *Manila in Europe*
Peter Mair *Partyless Democracy*
Tessa Morris-Suzuki *The Ambiguity of NGOs*
Michael Maar *Ordeal by Fire and Water*
Franco Moretti *New York Times*

David Marquand *From Baldwin to Blair*
Anthony Barnett *New Labour at Sea*
Nancy Fraser *Rethinking Recognition*
Georgi Derluguian *A Tale of Two Cities*
Peter Wollen *Government by Appearances*

SUBSCRIBE NOW to receive a FREE BOOK and FREE BACK ISSUE

One year's subscription for only £30!
—students pay only £20—

Special new series offer:
FREE BOOK and FREE BACK ISSUE
(tick one of each)

- ❏ Justin Rosenberg, *The Follies of Globalization Theory*
- ❏ Benedict Anderson, *The Spectre of Comparisons*
- ❏ Georg Lukács, *A Defence of History and Class Consciousness*

- ❏ NLR 7
- ❏ NLR 6
- ❏ NLR 5
- ❏ NLR 4
- ❏ NLR 3
- ❏ NLR 2

Annual subscription (6 issues): individuals £30/$50, institutions £60/$100, students £20/$35 (proof required).
Airmail: individuals £40/$65, institutions £70/$120.

Name
Address
Postcode

Cheques payable to New Left Review or Credit Card type:
_____ *(Access/Visa/Mastercard/Eurocard).* Expiry date _____
No: | | | | | | | | | | | | | | | |

Credit card hotline: +44 (0) 20 7434 1210; fax: +44 (0) 20 7439 3869
New Left Review, 6 Meard Street, London W1F 0EG, UK
email: subs@newleftreview.org

BERTRAND RUSSELL
from Routledge

The Selected Letters of Bertrand Russell
The Public Years 1914-1970

Edited by Nicholas Griffin, McMaster University, USA

This exciting selection reveals many letters never published before. Readers discover the inner workings of a philosophical genius and an impassioned campaigner for peace and social reform. The letters cover most of Russell's adult life, a period in which he wrote over thirty books, including his famous *History of Western Philosophy*. Richly illustrated with photographs from Russell's life, this volume includes letters to Ho Chi Minh, Tito, Jawahral Nehru and Jean-Paul Sartre.

Publication: May 2001: 688pages: Hb: 0-415-24998-8: **£25.00**

Common Sense and Nuclear Warfare
Bertrand Russell

Introduction by Ken Coates, Chairman of the Bertrand Russell Peace Foundation

'Russell's eloquent and lucid analyses and warnings ... should find a prominent place in the thinking of those who hope to reverse the seemingly inexorable drive towards self-destruction.' - *Noam Chomsky*

April 2001: 198x129: 240pp
Hb: 0-415-24994-5: **£45.00**
Pb: 0-415-24995-3: **£8.99**

Freedom and Organisation, 1814-1914
Bertrand Russell

This revealing account charts the struggle between two determining forces in nineteenth century history: freedom and control. Russell's text sweeps from the defeat of Napoleon and the Congress of Vienna to the lead up to the First World War.

April 2001: 216x138: 352pp
Hb: 0-415-24999-6: **£45.00**
Pb: 0-415-25000-5: **£10.99**

The Scientific Outlook
Bertrand Russell

With a new preface by David Papineau

'A scientific opinion is one which there is some reason to believe is true; an unscientific opinion is one which is held for some reason other than its probable truth.'
Bertrand Russell

April 2001: 198x129: 264pp
Hb: 0-415-24996-1: **£45.00**
Pb: 0-415-24997-X: **£9.99**

AVAILABLE FROM ALL GOOD BOOKSHOPS
For further information or a free catalogue,
call **020 7842 2149** or email **info.philosophy@routledge.co.uk**
UK and Europe: to order direct call +44 (0)8700 768853 or e-mail orders@routledge.co.uk
US and Canada: to order direct call 1-800-634-7064 or cserve@routledge-ny.com

www.philosophyArena.com

The Current Crises in the Middle East

What can we do?

Noam Chomsky

Noam Chomsky gave this lecture at the Massachusetts Institute of Technology. It was transcribed and edited in February 2001 by Angie D'Urso.

MIT must be relaxing its standards if this many people can show up right on the eve of finals.

Just how dangerous is the crisis in the Middle East? There is a UN Special Envoy, a Norwegian, Roed-Larson. A couple of days ago, he warned that Israel's blockade of the Palestinian areas is leading to enormous suffering and could rapidly detonate a regional war.

Notice that he referred to the blockade. He didn't refer to the killings, and the other atrocities. And he's right about that. The blockade is the crucial tactic. There can be a blockade which is very effective because of the way the so-called 'peace' process has evolved under US direction, meaning hundreds of isolated Palestinian enclaves, some of them tiny, which can be blocked off and strangled by the Israeli occupying forces. That's the basic structure of what's called here the peace process. So, there can be an extremely effective blockade. And a blockade is a sensible tactic for the United States and Israel, and they are always together. Remember that almost anything that Israel does, it does by US authorisation, and usually subsidy and support.

The blockade is a tactic to fine-tune the atrocities so that they don't become too visible, visible enough to force Washington or the West (which means Washington essentially) to make some kind of response.

There have been mistakes in the past and the United States and Israel have certainly learned from them. So, in 1996 for example, when Shimon Peres launched yet another attack on Lebanon, killing large numbers of people and driving hundreds of thousands out of their homes, it was fine, and the US was able to support it and Clinton did support it, up until one mistake, when they bombed a UN Camp in Qana, killing over a hundred people who were refugees in the camp. Clinton at first justified it, but as the international reaction came in, he had to back off, and Israel was forced, under US orders in effect, to call off the operation and withdraw. That's the kind of mistake you want to avoid. So, for those of you going into the diplomatic service, you can't allow that kind of mistake to happen. You want low level atrocities, fine-tuned, so that an international response is unnecessary. [Laughter]

The same thing happened more recently, just a year ago, last September, when the US-backed slaughter in East Timor, which had been going on nicely for about 25 years, finally got out of hand to such a degree that Clinton was compelled, after the country was virtually destroyed, to essentially tell the Indonesian generals that the game is over, and they instantly withdrew. So *that*, you want to avoid. In this particular case, there is a clear effort to keep killings, which is what hits the front pages, at roughly the level of Kosovo before the NATO bombing – in fact, that's about the level of killings right now – so that the story will sort of fade into the background.

Now, of course, the Kosovo story was quite different. At that time, the propaganda needs were the opposite. The killings were under fairly similar circumstances and the level of Serbian response was approximately like Israel's response in the occupied territories. (Then, in fact, there were attacks from right across the border, so it would be as if Hizbollah was carrying out attacks in the Galilee, or something like that). That time, the propaganda needs were different so, therefore, it was described passionately as genocide. A well designed propaganda system can make those distinctions. So in that case it was genocide, and in this case it's unnoticeable and justified reprisal.

The general idea, and I think you can expect this to continue for a while, is for the tactics to be restricted to: assassination; lots and lots of people wounded (severely – many of them will die later, but that doesn't enter into consciousness); starvation(according to the UN, there are about 600,000 people facing starvation, but again that is below the attention level for client states; and curfews (24 hour curfews, like in Hebron, for weeks at a time, while a couple of hundred Israeli settlers strut around freely, but the rest of the population, tens of thousands of people, are locked in their homes, allowed out a couple of hours a week).

The isolation in the hundreds of enclaves, and so on, is so that suffering can be kept below the level that might elicit a Western response. And the assumption, which is pretty plausible, is that there is a limit to what people can endure, and ultimately they will give up.

Well, there is, however, a problem in the Arab world, which is more sensitive to these massive atrocities, and it could explode, and that's what Roed-Larson is warning about. The governance in the Arab world is extremely fragile, especially in the crucial oil producing region. Any popular unrest might threaten the very fragile rule of the US clients, which the US would be unwilling to accept. And it might, equally unacceptably, induce the rulers of the oil monarchies to move to improve relations particularly with Iran (which, in fact, they've already been doing), which would undermine the whole framework for US domination of the world's major energy reserves.

Back in 1994, Clinton's National Security Advisor, Anthony Lake, described what he called a paradigm for the post Cold War era, and for the Middle East. The paradigm was what's called 'dual containment': the US contains Iraq and Iran. But dual containment relies crucially on the Oslo process, the process that brings about relative peace between Israel and the Arabs. Unless that can be sustained, the dual containment can't be sustained, and the whole US current policy for controlling the region will be in serious danger. That's happened already. Just two years ago in December 1998, the US and Britain bombed Iraq with outright and very explicit contempt for world opinion, including the UN Security Council. Remember that the bombing was timed just at the moment when the Security Council was having an emergency session to consider the problems of inspection in Iraq, and as they began, they got the announcement that the US and Britain had pre-empted it by bombing. That, and the events before it, elicited a very negative reaction in the Arab world, and elsewhere for that matter, and did lead to very visible steps, particularly by the Saudi ruling monarchy, but also others, towards accommodation to Iran, and indication of some degree of acceptance of an Iranian position that has been around for a while, that there should be a strategic alliance in the region that's independent of Western (meaning primarily US) power. That is something that the US is highly unlikely to accept and could lead to very dangerous consequences.

Furthermore, the countries in the region, Iran and Syria in particular, are testing missiles which might be able to reach Israel. The United States and Israel are working not only on missiles, but also on an anti-missile system, the Arrow anti-missile system. When armaments are at that level, tensions can easily break out suddenly and unpredictably and lead to a war with advanced weapons, which can get out of hand pretty quickly.

How dangerous is that? Turn to another expert, General Lee Butler, recently retired. He was head of the Strategic Command – the highest agency concerned with nuclear weapons – under Clinton, STRATCOM. He wrote a couple of years ago that 'it is dangerous in the extreme that in the cauldron of animosities that we call the Middle East, one nation has armed itself, ostensibly, with stockpiles of nuclear weapons, perhaps numbering in the hundreds, and that inspires other nations to do so,' and also to develop other weapons of mass destruction as a deterrent, which is highly combustible and can lead to very dangerous outcomes. All of this is still more dangerous when the sponsor of that one nation is regarded generally in the world as a rogue state, which is unpredictable and out of control, irrational and vindictive, and insists on portraying itself in that fashion. In fact, the Strategic Command under Clinton has, in its highest level pronouncements, advised that the United States should maintain a national persona, as they call it, of being irrational and vindictive and out of control so that the rest of the world will be frightened. And they are. And they advised further that the US should also rely on nuclear weapons as the core of its strategy, including the right of first use against non-nuclear states, including those that have signed the Non-Proliferation Treaty. Those proposals have been built into presidential directives, Clinton-era presidential directives, that don't make much noise around here, but it is understood in the world, which is naturally impelled to respond by developing weapons of mass destruction of its own in self defence. These prospects are recognised by US intelligence and high level US analysts. About two years ago, Harvard professor Samuel Huntington wrote an article in a very prestigious journal, *Foreign Affairs*, in which he pointed out that in much of the world, he indicated most of the world, the United States is considered a dangerous rogue state, and the main threat to their national existence. And it's not surprising, if you look at what happens in the world from outside the framework of the US indoctrination system. That's very plausible even from documents, and certainly from actions, and much of the world does see it that way, and that adds to the severe dangers of the situation.

The recent history of the Middle East provides quite a few further warnings. I'll just mention one example, which is very crucial in the present context right now – that's 1967. In the June 1967 war when Israel destroyed the Arab armies, the armies of the Arab states, Egypt most importantly, and it conquered the currently occupied territories. That set the stage for what's still going on right now. At that time, the Soviet Union was still around, and the conflict there became serious enough so that it almost led to a war – a nuclear war, which would have been the end of the story. Then Defence Secretary Robert McNamara later observed, in his words, 'we damned near had war'. At the end of the June war there were hot line communications, apparently Prime Minister Kosygin warned that if you want to have war, you can have it. There were naval confrontations between the Russian and the US fleets in the Eastern Mediterranean.

There was also another case. There was an Israeli attack on a US spy ship, USS *Liberty*, which killed about 35 sailors and crewmen and practically sank the ship. The *Liberty* didn't know who was attacking it. The attackers were disguised. Before they were disabled, they got messages back to the 6th Fleet Headquarters in Naples, who also didn't know who was attacking it. They sent out Phantoms, which were nuclear-armed, because they didn't have any that weren't nuclear-armed, to respond to whoever was attacking it, and they didn't know who they were supposed to bomb – Russia, Egypt, you know, anybody. Apparently the planes were called back directly from the Pentagon at the last moment. But that event alone could have lead to a nuclear war.

All of this was understood to be extremely hazardous. Most of this probably had to do with Israel's plans to conquer the Golan Heights, which they did after the ceasefire. And they didn't want the United States to know about it in advance because the US would have stopped them, and probably that's what lies behind most of this. Documents aren't out, so we can only speculate, and they will probably never come out. Anyhow, the situation was ominous enough so that the great powers on all sides figured that they better put a stop to it, and they very quickly met at the Security Council and accepted a resolution, UN 242, the famous UN 242 from November 1967, which laid out a framework for a diplomatic settlement.

And it's worth paying close attention to what UN 242 was and is. It's different now from what it was then. The information about this is public technically, but barely known and often distorted, so just pay attention to what it is. You can easily check it if you like.

The basic idea of UN 242 was full peace in return for a full withdrawal. So, Israel would withdraw from the territories that it just conquered, and in return, the Arab states would agree to a full peace with it. There was kind of a minor footnote, that the withdrawal could involve minor and mutual adjustments. So, for example, regarding some line or curve, they could straighten it out, that sort of thing. But that was the policy, and that was US policy – it was under US initiative. So, full peace in return for full withdrawal. Notice that this very crucially, and it's very crucial now, that UN 242 was completely 'rejectionist'.

I use the term 'rejectionist' now in a slightly non-standard sense, in a non-racist sense. It is usually used in a completely racist sense. So the rejectionists are those who deny Israel's right to national self-determination. But, of course, there are two national groups contesting, and I am using the term rejectionist in a neutral sense, hence non-standard, to refer to a denial of the rights of either of the two contestants, including denials of Palestinian rights. That terminology is never used in the United States, and can't be used, because if it is used, it will turn out that the United States is the leader of the rejectionist camp, and we can't have that. So therefore the term is always used in a racist sense. So, you will understand that I'm switching from normal usage now.

UN 242 was completely rejectionist. It offered nothing to the Palestinians. There was no reference to them, except the phrase that there was a refugee problem that somehow had to be dealt with. That's it. Apart from that, it was to be an agreement among the states. The states were to reach full peace treaties in the context of complete Israeli withdrawal from the territories. That's UN 242.

For the local people in the region, the Israelis and the Palestinians, the crisis is obviously extremely grave. It could lead to a regional war that could easily escalate to a global war with weapons of mass destruction with consequences that are unimaginable, and that could happen at almost any time.

Secondly, the US role is highly significant. That's always true throughout the world just because of US power, but it's particularly true in the Middle East, which has been recognised in high level planning for 50 years (and goes back beyond that, but explicitly for 50 years) as a core element in US global planning. Just to quote documents from 50 years ago, declassified documents, the Middle East was described as the 'strategically most important region of the world', 'a stupendous source of strategic power', 'the richest economic prize in the world', and, you know, on and on in the same vein. The US is not going to give that up. And the reason is very simple. That's the world's major energy reserves, and not only are they valuable to have because of the enormous profit that comes from them, but control over them gives a kind of veto power over the actions of others for obvious reasons, which was recognised right away at the time. So, that's a core issue. It's been the prime concern of US military and strategic planning for half a century. The Gulf region, the region of major energy reserves, has always been the target of the major US intervention forces, with a base system that extends over a good part of the world, from the Pacific to the Azores, with consequences for all of those regions because they are back-up bases for the intervention forces targeting the Gulf region, also including the Indian Ocean.

And this is a big issue right now, in England at least, and much of the world, but not in the United States. The inhabitants of an Indian Ocean island, Diego Garcia, were kicked out and unceremoniously dumped on another island, Mauritius, some years ago, and those who managed to survive it have been fighting through the British Courts (this was a British dependency) to try to gain the right to return to their homes. They finally won a couple of months ago in the High Court in England and were granted the right to return, except that the US won't relinquish the island, where it has a major military base that's used for the Middle East-targeted forces. Just a couple of days ago, they asked for indemnity of about 6 billion dollars, and the US is refusing to pay up, of course. Madeleine Albright commented on it. She said it's just an issue between Britain and Mauritius. We don't have anything to do with it, even though we hold the island and refuse to allow them to return, and refuse to pay indemnities. I think you'll search pretty far to find some discussion of this in the US press, but that's part of the base system for targeting the Middle East.

For years, there was a kind of a public pretext for all of this. The public pretext was that we had to defend ourselves against the Russians. That was the pretext for everything, and the pretext for this in particular. There is a pretty rich internal record which tells quite a different story, however. The story it tells is that the Russians were, at most, a marginal factor, often no factor. But, fortunately, there is no need to debate the matter anymore because it has been conceded publicly. It was conceded, in fact, immediately after the fall of the Berlin Wall, which sort of got rid of the pretext. You can't appeal to the Russian threat anymore.

A couple of weeks after the fall of the Berlin Wall, the Bush Administration submitted its annual message to Congress, calling for a huge military budget, and it was a very interesting document. Unfortunately it wasn't reported, but it was very important obviously – the first call for a huge military budget after the fall of the Berlin Wall, when you can't appeal to the Russians anymore. So, therefore, it's revealing and tells you what's really going on. As expected, the Russian threat was gone. We don't need a huge Pentagon budget because of the Russians who aren't around anymore, but we still need it. In fact, it turned out to be exactly as it was in the past, and we needed it for reasons which are now frankly expressed. We needed it because of what they called the technological sophistication of Third World countries, which is a way of saying they pose a danger of becoming independent. And, we need it because we have to maintain what's called the defence industrial base, which is what pays our salaries among other things. The defence industrial base is just a term for hi-tech industry, which has to be funded by the public, which has to bear the costs and risks of development. MIT is one of the funnels for that. That has to be maintained. We have to keep the source of the dynamic sectors of the economy, which are substantially in the public sector, so we have to maintain the defence industrial base. And we also have to keep the intervention forces that we've always had still targeting the Middle East, the Gulf region. Then it adds the interesting phrase: 'where the threat to our interests that involves possible military action could not be laid at the Kremlin's door' – contrary to half a century, forty years, of lies. Sorry folks, we've been lying to you, but we still need them there because of the technological sophistication of Third World powers, that is, the threat that they may become independent.

Notice that the threat to our interests could also not be laid at Iraq's door at that time because Saddam Hussein was still a nice guy. He had only been gassing Kurds, and torturing dissidents, and that sort of thing. But he was considered obedient, so he was a friend and ally. This is early 1990. It changed a few months later.

So, we don't have to debate the question of the Russian threat. It's now conceded that that was not a significant threat, could not be laid at the Kremlin's door, and the threat, in fact, is what it is all over the world, and has been right through the Cold War, the threat of what's called 'radical nationalism' or 'independent nationalism'. It doesn't make much of a difference where it is in the political spectrum. But, if it's independent, it's a danger and you have to undermine it as a way of maintaining what's called stability, that is, the subordination to the dominant interests that the US represents.

US relations with Israel developed in that context. The 1967 war was a major step forward, when Israel showed its power and ability to deal with Third World radical nationalists, who were, at that time, threatening, particularly Nasser. Nasser was engaged in a kind of proxy war with Saudi Arabia, which is the most important country, that's where all the oil is, in the Yemen. And Israel put an end to that by smashing Nasser's armies and won a lot of points for that, and US relations with Israel really became solidified at that point. But it had been recognised 10 years earlier. US intelligence had noted that what they called 'a logical corollary' to opposition to radical Arab nationalism is support for Israel as a reliable base for US power in the region. And Israel is reliable because it's under threat, and therefore it needs US support, which has another logical corollary, that for US interests it's a good idea for Israel to be under threat. That essentially continues, and a good deal of the relationship is based on the way that context developed.

Anyhow, we can thankfully put the pretext aside at this point, and just look at the reasons which are now on the table – it's the threat of independent nationalism, and in the case of the Gulf region, that's particularly important because that's the world's major energy reserves.

The final consideration, before we move on to the topic at hand, is that the US role -- though not the only one, of course; it's one factor in a complicated mixture – is nevertheless a decisive factor, and crucially, it's the one factor that's under our control. We can directly influence it. So, we can bewail the terrible actions of other people, but we can do something about our own actions. That's a rather critical difference, in personal life and in international affairs. And it's illuminating to observe how much attention is given to the crimes of others, which most of the time we can't do anything about, and compare it with the amount of attention that is given to our own crimes, which we can do a great deal about. That's an instructive comparison, and if you take the trouble to work it out, you learn a lot about the intellectual culture in which we live and to which we're expected to contribute. For that reason alone, and it's far from the only one, we ought to be discussing primarily the US role. And furthermore, that role is little understood. It's often just suppressed, which is another reason to focus on it.

Let me illustrate with some of the things that are happening right at this moment. The *Intifada*, the current uprising, began on September 29th, that was the day after General Ariel Sharon appeared at the Haram al Sharif with a lot of troops. That event alone was provocative, but it probably would have gone by without any reaction. What happened the next day, however, was different. The next day is Friday, the day of prayers, and there was a huge military presence, mostly border guards who are kind of like the paramilitaries, the ones you farm out atrocities to, and they were there in force, and as people came out of the Mosques, it was obviously extremely provocative. Some rock throwing took place. They shot into the crowds, killed four or more people, wounded over a hundred. And after that, it just took off. This is incidentally Barak, not Sharon. It's easy to blame Sharon, and there's plenty to blame on him for fifty years of atrocities, but this happened to be Barak's planning.

Let me just consider one aspect of what has gone on since: the use of helicopter gunships. On October 1st, right after this, Israel military helicopters, meaning US helicopters with Israeli pilots, killed two Palestinians in Gaza. On October 2nd, the next day, they killed 10 Palestinians, wounded 35 others in Gaza at Netzarim, which if you follow this closely, you'll notice is the scene of many of the major atrocities, including the famous photo of the 12 year old boy who was killed. What's Netzarim? Well, the fact is, Netzarim is just an excuse to split the Gaza Strip in two. There's a small settlement south of Gaza, the only purpose of which is to require a big military outpost to protect it, and the military outpost then requires a road, a huge road, which cuts the Gaza Strip in two, so that separates Gaza City, the main population concentration, from the Southern part of the strip, and Egypt, and insures that if any problem arises, Gaza will be imprisoned inside Israel in effect. There are other breaks down farther south, but Netzarim is the main one, and that is where a lot of the atrocities have been. So this October 2nd killing of 10 and wounding of 35 at Netzarim by helicopters is just one of these many incidents.

On October 3rd, the next day, the Defence Correspondent of *Ha'aretz*, which is the major serious Hebrew newspaper, reported the largest purchase of military helicopters in a decade – that means US military helicopters. These were Blackhawks, and spare parts for Apaches. Apaches are the main attack helicopters. These had been delivered a few weeks earlier. They were getting spare parts, also jet fuel.

The next day, October 4th, *Jane's Defence Weekly*, which is the major military journal in the world, the British military journal, reported that the Clinton administration had further approved a new sale of attack helicopters, Apache attack helicopters, because they had decided that upgrading the ones that they had just sent would not be sufficient, so they really had to send new, more advanced ones. The same day the *Boston Globe* reported that Apache attack helicopters were attacking apartment complexes with rockets, again in Netzarim. The international press agencies at that time quoted Pentagon officials as saying, and I'm quoting a Pentagon official, 'US weapon sales do not carry a stipulation that the weapons cannot be used against civilians. We cannot second guess an Israeli commander who calls in helicopter gunships.' Okay, so, the story so far – US helicopter gunships are being used to attack civilians, but they aren't advanced enough, and Israel doesn't have enough of them, so therefore, the Clinton Administration had to move in with the biggest purchase in a decade. Purchase means American taxpayers pay for it in some indirect fashion. And then it had the next day to extend it further, sending them more advanced Apache helicopters, and there's no stipulation going along with them that they can't be used against civilians. That carries us up to October 4th. Then come more and more attacks on civilians.

The first reference in the US press to any of this is on October 12th. There was an opinion piece in the Raleigh North Carolina newspaper, which said they thought this was kind of a bad idea. That's also the last reference to it in the US press, meaning the only reference. It's not that editors don't know about this. Of course they know about it. In fact, it has been explicitly brought to the attention of editors of leading newspapers, as if they didn't know already. And it's not that it's unimportant, because it is obviously very important. It's just the kind of news that's not fit to print. And that's very typical, not only in this part of the world, but everywhere. It's extremely important that the public be kept in the dark about what's being done, because if they know about it, they're not going to like it. And if they don't like it, they might do something about it. So, there's a grave responsibility on the media, and on intellectuals generally, the educational system and so on, to ensure that people are kept in the dark about things that it's better for them not to know, like this for example. And the task is carried out with very impressive dedication. This is not an untypical example.

On October 19th, Amnesty International published a report condemning the United States for providing new military helicopters to Israel. They were also reporting the atrocities. That was not reported in the United States. It was elsewhere.

On November 10th, Amnesty International published a much broader condemnation of the excessive use of force and terror, and so on, that was barely mentioned. So it continues.

Let's turn to the question, what can we do? The answer is we have choices. We can do a lot. So, for example, we can continue to provide helicopter gunships and other military support to ensure that Israel is able to attack civilians, maintain a blockade, starve them to death, and so on. And we can provide the funding that allows Israel to continue to integrate the occupied territories within Israel proper as it has been doing, settlements, infrastructure, etc. It doesn't matter which government is in office. It goes on under Barak about the same way it did under Netanyahu. And it's anticipated to go on next year. The budget provisions have already been made for next year. So we can continue with that if we'd like. Or, we can act to stop our participation in these activities, which is pretty straightforward. It doesn't require bombing or sanctions. It just means stop participating in atrocities, the easiest thing to do. That's a choice. And, in fact, we may even go further and call them off, as is pretty easily done when a country has the power that the United States has. I gave a couple of examples.

If we decide on the latter choice, which is always open here and elsewhere, there's a prerequisite. The prerequisite is that we know what's going on. So you can't make that choice, say to stop providing military helicopters (and you know the helicopters are just an illustration of a much bigger picture) unless you know about it. Again, the grave responsibility of the intellectual world, the media, journals, universities, and others, is to prevent people from knowing. That takes effort. It's not easy. As in this case, it takes some dedication to suppress the facts and make sure that the population doesn't know what's being done in their name, because if they do, they aren't going to like it, and they'll respond. Then you get into trouble.

The very same applies to the diplomatic record. Let me turn to that. Let's begin with the current phase of diplomacy, which started in September 1993, that's the famous Oslo process. In September 1993, there was a meeting on the White House lawn, very august, with the *Boston Globe* having a headline describing it as 'a day of awe'. The Israelis and the Palestinians agreed, under Clinton's supervision, to what's called a Declaration of Principles. There were at that time a number of issues, and it's crucial to understand how the Declaration of Principles dealt with them.

One issue was territory – what's going to happen with the occupied territories, how they are going to be assigned – that's issue number one.

Number two is the issue of national rights. Now that issue only arises for Palestinians. There is no question in the case of Israel, that's just not in question and hasn't been in question at all. The only question is what about the rights of the Palestinians?

The third question is what about the right to resist? And do the Palestinians, or the Lebanese for that matter, have the right to resist military occupation. That's the third question.

The fourth question, which is kind of a counterpart to that, is whether the occupying power, Israel, (which means the US here) has the right to attack in the occupied territories and in Lebanon? Those are the four main questions.

There were answers in the Declaration of Principles. With regard to territory, the Declaration of Principles stated that the permanent settlement would be on the basis of UN 242, but that raises a question. What does UN 242 mean? Here, we have to go to the earlier diplomatic record. I'll return to it in a moment.

The second, with regard to national rights, again, is settled in terms of UN 242. And anyone who was paying attention in September 1993 could see exactly where this was going. The Declaration of Principles states that the permanent settlement, long term outcome, you know, the end of the road, will be based upon UN 242 alone. Now for 20 years, the issue in international diplomacy had been the rejectionism of UN 242. Remember, UN 242 says nothing about the Palestinians. For 20 years there has been a series of efforts by the whole world to supplement UN 242 to include Palestinian rights alongside the rights of Israel, which were never in question. That was the issue from the mid-70's right up until Oslo, and the US won flat out on that one. Palestinian rights are not to be considered. It's just UN 242, no Palestinian rights. They are not mentioned, and that's the permanent settlement. So, territories, it's UN 242, which means what the US decides (I'll come back to that), national rights – US wins flat out, the rest of the world capitulates. What about the right to resist?

Arafat agreed at the signing of the Declaration of Principles to abandon any right to resist, and it's taken for granted that in Lebanon the population also has no right to resist. It's called terrorism if they resist. Why did Arafat have to state this? He had actually said it over and over again. You know, he made solemn pronouncements to that effect over and over, but the purpose here was just pure humiliation. You have to make sure you humiliate the lower breeds to make sure that they don't get too big for their britches. George Shultz, Secretary of State, who is considered something of a dove, put it pretty plainly. He said it's true that Arafat has said unc, unc, unc, and he said le, le, le, but he hasn't said uncle, uncle, uncle in a sufficiently submissive tone, and we ought to make sure that he does, over and over again. That's the way you treat the lower breeds. So, once again, Arafat had to say uncle, loudly and submissively, and thank you Massa, and sign a statement saying, you know, once again, we reject the right to resist. Same in Lebanon, it isn't even a question.

What about the fourth question, the right to attack? A counterpart is Israel's right to attack. They've retained that right, and Israel continues to use it repeatedly with US support before and after. Notice that over this period there is virtually no defensive pretext, contrary to what you read in US commentary. That goes way back. But, contrary to propaganda, almost the entire series of US/Israeli attacks, certainly in the occupied territories, but in Lebanon as well, were not for any defensive purpose. They were initiated. That includes the 1982 invasion, and that's no small matter. I mean, it's not considered a big deal here, but during the 22 years that Israel illegally occupied Southern Lebanon in violation of Security Council orders (but with US authorisation), they killed about maybe 45,000 or 50,000 Lebanese and Palestinians. Not a trivial number. This included many very brutal attacks going on after the Oslo accords as well, in 1993, 1996, and so on.

Incidentally, you might again want to compare this with Serbia and Kosovo. The comparison in this case has to be kind of like a thought experiment, because it never happened. But, imagine if Serbia had been bombing Albania to the extent that Israel was bombing Lebanon, that would be an analogy. It didn't happen, but you can just imagine what the reaction would have been. It tells you again something about our values and of the need to maintain discipline on these issues, so that people don't think it through.

The PLO accepted all this, just abjectly. Israel in return in the Declaration of Principles committed itself to absolutely nothing. You should take a look back at what happened on the White House lawn, on 'the day of awe'. Prime Minister Rabin made a very terse comment, a couple of lines, in which, after Arafat agreed to all of this stuff, he said that Israel would now recognise the PLO as the representative of the Palestinians – period. Nothing about national rights. Nothing. We just recognise you as the representative of the Palestinians, and his Foreign Minister, Shimon Peres, considered a dove, explained why right away in Israel, in Hebrew. He said, well, yeah, we can recognise them now because they've capitulated, so there is no problem in recognising them. They can now become a kind of junior partner in controlling the Palestinian population, which follows a traditional colonial pattern.

Israel and the United States had made a rather serious error in the occupied territories. It's not a good idea to try to control a subject population with your own troops. The way it is usually done is, you farm it out to the natives. That's the way the British ran India for a couple of hundred years. India was mostly controlled by Indian troops, often taken from other regions, you know like the Gurkhas and so on. That's the way the United States runs Central America, with mercenary forces, which are called armies, if you can keep them under control. That's the way South Africa ran the Black areas. Most of the atrocities were carried out by Black mercenaries, and in the Bantustans, it was entirely Blacks. That's the standard colonial pattern and it makes a lot of sense. If you have your own troops out there, it causes all kinds of problems. You know, first of all they suffer injuries, and these are people who don't like to feel good about killing people, and their parents get upset and so on and so forth, but if you have mercenaries or paramilitaries, you don't have those problems. So, Israel and the United States were going to turn to the standard colonial pattern and have the Palestinian forces, who in fact mostly came from Tunis, control the local population – control them economically and politically, as well as militarily. That was the idea, a sensible reversion to standard colonial practice.

Let's move a little back to the earlier diplomatic record, which helps put all of this in context. So, what about the right to resist? The right to resist military occupation in the territories, and in Lebanon? That actually has been discussed in the international community, though you wouldn't know it here. In December 1987, which was right at the peak of all of the furore about international terrorism, you know, the plague of the modern world, and so on and so forth, the UN General Assembly considered and passed a resolution condemning terrorism very strongly: international terrorism is the worst crime there is, and had all of the right wording in it and so on and so forth. The resolution was passed 153 to

2, which is actually pretty normal. The two were the usual ones, the United States and Israel. One country only abstained, Honduras, for unknown reasons, so it was essentially unanimous except for the United States and Israel. Now, why would the United States and Israel reject, and that means veto since it's a US vote against a resolution denouncing terrorism? The reason is because it contained one paragraph which said that nothing in this resolution prejudices the right of people to struggle against racist and colonialist regimes and foreign military occupation and to gain the support of others for their struggle for freedom under these conditions. That, the US won't accept, of course. For example, that would have given the ANC in South Africa the right to resist the South African regime, which is unacceptable. It would have given the Lebanese the right to resist Israeli military occupation and attacks, which can't be accepted, and it would have extended to the occupied territories as well. So, therefore, the US and Israel rejected it, and in fact, as usual, it is vetoed from history. It was never reported here, it was never mentioned, it might as well not exist unless you read dissident literature. It's there, I mean if you go to the UN's dusty records you can find it. But that's the right to resist, which was blocked by the United States in 1987 and is out of history.

What about the right to attack? Well, that exists by US fiat, as I mentioned, during the 22 years of Israeli occupation of Southern Lebanon. With US authorisation, they killed tens of thousands of people, probably 40,000 to 50,000, and there are plenty of atrocities, Peres's terrorist iron fist operations in 1985 for example. But, it's not only there. The right extends much further. So 1985 and 1986 are interesting years. That was the peak of the hysteria about international terrorism. And, in fact, there was plenty of international terrorism in those years. For example, in 1985 Israel bombed Tunis, killing 75 people, Tunisians and Palestinians, with no credible pretext. The United States publicly backed it, although Shultz, then Secretary of State, backed off when the Security Council condemned it unanimously as an act of armed aggression, namely a war crime, with the US abstaining. The US was directly involved. The 6th Fleet in the Mediterranean sort of pulled back so that the Israeli planes would be able to refuel with the 6th Fleet pretending not to notice them, and the United States did not warn Tunisia, an ally, that this bombing attack was coming. So that's a major act of terrorism outside the local area of the Middle East, and there are many others. In fact, the main act of terrorism in that year, sort of garden variety terrorism, was a car bombing in Beirut which killed 80 people and wounded about 200, set off by the CIA, British Intelligence, and Saudi Intelligence, in an effort to kill a Muslim cleric who they missed, but they got a lot of other people. It was a car bombing right outside a mosque, timed to go off right when everybody would be coming out, so you get maximum killing of civilians. That's there, but also not in the annals of terrorism, any more than the bombing of Tunis, or for example, the US bombing of Libya the next year, which is another act of armed aggression, but considered okay.

I should say that Arab opinion in the Middle East, and here too, is very misled about all this in my opinion. It very consistently, if you read it now or in the past, claims that the United States overlooks Israeli terrorism because of the Jewish influence or Jewish lobby, or something like that. And this is simply untrue. It's missing the fact that a much more general principle applies to this case and to many others. The principle is that the United States has the right of terrorism and that right is inherited by its clients, and it doesn't matter who they are. So, Israel happens to be a US client, so it inherits the right of terror.

And you can see this very easily in other parts of the world. Just to give one illustration from a different part of the world at the same time, 1987. The State Department conceded what anyone paying attention knew that the US terrorist forces attacking Nicaragua were being directed, commanded, and trained to attack what were called 'soft' targets, meaning defenceless civilian targets, like agricultural co-operatives and health centres and so on. And they were able to do this because the US had total control of the air, and surveillance, and was able to communicate the position of the Nicaraguan army forces to the local terrorist forces attacking from Honduras, so that they could attack somewhere else, and so on. That was all conceded publicly, but nobody paid much attention except those who are interested in these things. But the human rights groups did protest. Americas Watch protested against this, and said this was really awful.

And there was a response – an interesting response, that you should read – by Michael Kinsley, who was a kind of representative of the dovish left in mainstream commentary, and still is. He had an article in which he pointed out, speaking from the dovish left, that it's perfectly true that these terrorist attacks against undefended targets, in his words, 'caused vast civilian suffering' but they may nevertheless be sensible and legitimate. The way we decide this is by carrying out 'cost benefit analysis', namely, and I'm quoting all through this, we have to measure 'the amount of blood and misery that we will be pouring in' and compare it with the outcome, you know, democracy in our sense, meaning rule by the business world with the population crushed. And if the cost benefit analysis comes out okay, then it's right to pour in blood and misery and cause vast suffering. In short, aggression and terror have to meet a pragmatic criterion, and we are the ones who decide whether it's met, not anybody else, and US clients inherit that right – and it doesn't have to be Israel. It can be anybody else. So, it can be Arabs for example. Saddam Hussein is a striking case. In 1988 remember, Saddam Hussein was still a loyal friend and ally, and that's when he committed his worst crimes; the gassing of the Kurds, and so on. The US thought that was okay and they continued to support him. They downplayed it, and provided him with dual use technology that could be used for military purposes and weapons of mass destruction, and also sent agricultural assistance which he badly needed. The Kurds were in an agricultural region, so Iraq was short of food, so the Bush Administration moved in with agricultural exports, a boon to US agribusiness as well, and that continued. In fact, Iraq, an Arab state, was allowed to do something that up until then only Israel had been allowed to do, namely, attack a US ship and kill sailors. Iraq was permitted to attack the USS

Stark, the destroyer, and kill 37 crewmen with missiles, and didn't even get a tap on the wrist. You're really privileged if you are allowed to do that. Up until then, the only country that had been allowed to do that was Israel in 1967 in the case of the USS *Liberty*. And remember, this is an Arab state. That was important. Again, nobody pays much attention here, but in the region people paid attention. In particular, Iran paid attention. This was part of what convinced Iran to capitulate to Iraq as the US wanted. The other major event that convinced Iran that the US was really serious was the shooting down of an Iranian airliner, killing 290 people in Iranian airspace. But that wasn't even a problem. Again it's kind of sloughed off here, not very important, but for the Iranians, that was important, and they understood from these acts that the US was going to go to any lengths to ensure that Saddam Hussein won, so they capitulated, not a small point in the politics of the region. Here, people don't want to think about it, but elsewhere in the world they do.

So, I think the thing to be recognised is, contrary to a lot of the Arab commentary abroad and here, Washington really is an equal opportunity employer. That is, it adheres pretty well to a policy of non-discrimination in advocacy of terror and war crimes, and so on. Other issues are involved, not, you know, who you are.

Let's go a couple of steps back further, to 242. Remember that UN 242, the basic document and the permanent settlement according to the current process, was strictly rejectionist, nothing for the Palestinians. It was taken really seriously. There was a threat of war at the time, nuclear war. It called for full peace in return for full withdrawal. There was a deadlock. Israel refused full withdrawal, the Arab states refused full peace. That deadlock was broken in 1971, when President Sadat of Egypt, who had just come into office, offered to accept the official US position. So, he said, yeah, he'll accept full peace with Israel in return for partial withdrawal, didn't even go as far as 242, namely withdrawal from Egyptian territory. So, if Israel would withdraw from the Sinai, Sadat would agree to full peace. Didn't say anything about the Palestinians, nothing about the West Bank. Israel recognised that officially in response as a genuine peace offer. Rabin in his memoirs later called it a 'famous milestone' on the path to peace.

Internally in Israel it was understood that they could have peace at this point, general peace. One of the leading Labour Party officials, a retired general, Haim Bar-Lev, wrote in a Labour Party journal at the time that with this offer we can have full peace. The conflict's over, if we decide it's over, but I think we should refuse, because if we hold out, we can get more. This would require us to withdraw from the Sinai, and I don't think we have to. So therefore, we should hold out and abandon peace, and that's what Israel did. Its response was that it would not withdraw to the pre-June borders.

The US was then in a dilemma. Should it continue with its official policy, the policy which in fact it had initiated, UN 242, and that means siding with Sadat-Egypt against Israel, or should it abandon its policy and side with Israel against

Egypt, but that means rescinding UN 242 in effect? And there was an internal conflict. The State Department was in favour of keeping to this policy. Kissinger, National Security Advisor, wanted what he called stalemate, meaning no diplomacy, no negotiations, just force. And in the internal conflict, Kissinger won out. The US effectively rescinded UN 242, which no longer exists. And people should understand that.

UN 242 now means what the United States says it means, as do other things, that's the meaning of power. It means withdrawal, insofar as the US and Israel determine, and that's what it's meant ever since. So when Palestinians or Arab states now complain that Israel isn't living up to 242, they are just choosing to ignore the historical record, and blindness is not a helpful position in world affairs. You might as well have your eyes open. UN 242 since February 1971 does not exist. It exists only in the Kissingerian sense. Now, here you have to be a little nuanced, because officially the US continues to endorse UN 242 in its original sense. So you can find statements by Jimmy Carter and Ronald Reagan, or speechwriters, and George Bush, saying yeah, we insist on 242 in its original sense. You can't find statements by Clinton. Clinton, I think, is the first president not even having given lip service to it. But the fact is that the lip service is pure hypocrisy, because while they are adhering to it for public purposes, they are also providing Israel with the wherewithal, the funds, the military support, the diplomatic support, to violate it, namely to act to integrate the occupied territories within Israel, so the endorsement of it is hypocritical and you should compliment Clinton on having the honesty simply to withdraw it, in effect.

That brings us up to February 1971. The United States has also blocked other UN resolutions, though it did continue to support UN resolution 194, December 11, 1948, which called for the right of return of refugees, or a compensation. That was technically endorsed by the United States, like they voted for it at the UN every year, but pure hypocrisy. And again Clinton overcame the hypocrisy. He withdrew support for it. So the last vote was unanimous with Israel and the United States opposed, and the Clinton Administration also declared all other related UN resolutions null and void. It will now only be the Oslo process, so that's honesty again.

Sadat in 1971 made it very clear, and continued for several years, to make it clear that if the United States refused to accept a negotiated settlement, he would be forced to go to war. Nobody took him seriously. A lot of racism here, it was assumed that Arabs didn't know which end of the gun to hold and that sort of thing. Finally war came in 1973, and it turned out to be a very close thing, and it scared everyone. There was another near nuclear confrontation and Israel was in deep trouble for a while. And it was understood that Egypt can't just be written off. They're not just a basket case. So, Kissinger moved to the natural fall back position, namely exclude Egypt from the conflict. It's the only Arab deterrent, so we can't just ignore it, so exclude it from the conflict. Then follows shuttle diplomacy. In 1977 comes Sadat's famous trip to Jerusalem, where he was hailed as a kind of a saint for being the first Arab leader to be willing to talk to Israel.

In fact, in Jerusalem, if you look at his speech, it was less forthcoming than his offer in February 1971. In February 1971, he offered full peace, with nothing about the Palestinians. In his trip to Jerusalem, he insisted on rights for the Palestinians. But that's allowed to enter history. February 1971 is out of history. I mean you often can't even find it in the scholarly literature. But, the trip to Jerusalem is in history because at that time the US was compelled to accept the offer, whereas in February of 1971 it was able to reject the offer. So one is out of history, the other is in history. Sadat is a secular saint because of his trip in 1977, not because of his more forthcoming offer in February 1971.

That goes on to Camp David in 1978 and 1979, under Carter, and it's considered a grand moment of the peace process. Israel did agree to withdraw from Sinai as Egypt had offered seven years earlier, and the US at this point had no choice but to agree. The result, however, was understood very clearly in Israel. One leading Israeli military strategic analyst, Avner Yaniv, pointed out right away that the Camp David settlement eliminates the only Arab deterrent and therefore allows Israel to continue at will to integrate the occupied territories into Israel and to attack its northern neighbour, to attack Lebanon, with massive US support in both cases. The Carter Administration rapidly increased support to more than half of the total US aid overseas, making sure that these ends could be achieved.

While all this was going on, there was another current. The international consensus on the issue had shifted. In 1967, there was nothing for the Palestinians, no Palestinian rights. By the early 70s that was changing. By the mid-70s there was an extremely broad international consensus, including just about everybody, calling for Palestinian national rights, alongside of Israel. It included the Russians, it included Europe, it included Asia, Latin America, virtually everyone.

That came to a head in January 1976, another very important event, crucial for understanding what's happening now, but out of history, because it tells the wrong story. You can find it, but you know, it's out of history, again even out of scholarship. In January 1976, the United Nations Security Council considered a resolution calling for a two state settlement. It included all the wording of UN 242, so everything about Israel's rights and so on, but it added national rights for the Palestinians in the territories that had been occupied, from which Israel was to withdraw according to the original understanding of 242. What happened to that? That resolution was actually brought by what are called the confrontation states, Syria, Egypt, and Jordan. It was strongly supported by the PLO, though they may have forgotten that. In fact, I suspect they have. But, in fact, according to Israel's UN representative, Chaim Herzog, later President, the resolution was actually prepared by the PLO. I don't think that's likely, but that's what Israel perceives, at least. Anyhow, it was certainly supported by them, and by the confrontation states, and indeed, by virtually the entire world. Maybe Khaddafi didn't support it, I don't remember. But essentially the whole world supported it.

And Israel and the United States had to react. Israel reacted in a typical way, by bombing Lebanon. It bombed Lebanon, killing 50 people in some village that was chosen at random. That was reported here, but considered insignificant. It was retaliation against the United Nations, in effect. The United States reacted in a simpler way, namely by vetoing the resolution, and that means vetoed from history. Remember, it's very common for the US to veto Security Council resolutions. In fact, it's the champion of the world by a long shot. But they disappeared from history as well. Carter did the same thing in 1980, same resolution. But, meanwhile, the international consensus persisted.

Here you can begin to understand the significance of the fact that the Declaration of Principles in September of 1993 referred to UN 242 and nothing else. Because by then there is a whole raft of resolutions calling for Palestinian national rights, and they were not to be part of the permanent settlement under the US version of the peace process. The General Assembly had votes year after year, I won't run through the details. Their wording varied a little bit, but they were more or less the same, you know, kind of a two state settlement, national rights for both groups. The votes were 150 to 2, or something like that. Occasionally the US would pick up another vote, from El Salvador, or somebody, but that was year by year, essentially never reported. They will, in fact, probably never report it.

The last vote was December 1990, 144 to 2, and the date is important. Shortly after that, a couple of weeks after, the United States and Britain bombed Iraq. Saddam, remember, had shifted from loyal friend and ally to reincarnation of Hitler, not because of any crimes, the crimes were fine, but because he had disobeyed orders, or maybe misunderstood orders, and that's not permitted, so that's a standard transition, and therefore, you had to get rid of the beast of Baghdad, and it's obvious where the power was, so that worked. During the bombing, George Bush announced proudly the coming of the New World Order. He defined it very simply: 'What we say goes,' certainly with regard to the Middle East. The rest of the world understood that. Everybody backed off. Europe disappeared, the Third World was in disarray, Russia was gone.

At this point, the US could simply ram through its own extreme rejectionist position, and it did. The Madrid conference took place a few months later, and then you go straight on to Oslo. Then come successive agreements and the integration of the territories continues right through the Oslo period. The various agreements authorise this, the US funds it, it protects it diplomatically, which brings us up to Camp David and the year 2000.

Regarding the public discussion about Barak's remarkable offers – you know, forthcoming, willing to give away everything – there is absolutely no basis for any of that.

There was a focus on Jerusalem, and for good reasons. Jerusalem is probably the easiest of all of the problems to solve, and for Clinton and Barak it made good sense to focus on Jerusalem because then you would divert attention away from what's important, namely what's going on in the occupied territories, the settlements, the infrastructure development, the enclaves, and so on. For Arafat it also made good sense to focus on Jerusalem because he is desperately eager to get support from the Arab states, and the Arab states don't give a damn what happens to the Palestinians. Their populations may, but certainly not the leaders. On the other hand, they will find it difficult to abandon control over the religious sites, because if they do that, their populations will blow up. So, by focusing on the religious sites, it's kind of a negotiating ploy for Arafat, so they all focused on that, neglecting the crucial problem, what's going on elsewhere.

I have a couple of Israeli maps with me. These are final status maps, you know, what it's supposed to look like in the long term. Briefly, what's called Jerusalem extends almost all the way to the Jordan river, so that splits the West Bank in two, with a substantial city, Ma'ale Adumim, in the middle and extension all the way. There is another break in the North right through Samaria, includes towns that are settled there. Israel keeps the Jordan Valley, for the time being at least. Jericho is isolated. You end up with four Palestinian cantons, separated from one another, separated from Jerusalem. There's some hint that in the long term, some meaningless connection will be established between them, but they are essentially completely controlled and surrounded. What's called Jerusalem extends north of Ramallah, and south of Bethlehem. If you look at the map, that's the area which splits the northern and central and southern settlement areas. It's kind of modelled on South Africa's policies in the early 60s. The population concentrations should be under local administration, but everything else is taken over by the dominant power, the resources, the useable land, and so on. And there are massive infrastructure developments that sort of lie behind this.

The US is paying for all of it, of course. That's the marvellous offer that was given a few months ago at Camp David. And apart from what's talked about, what actually counts, of course, is what's happening on the ground. And what's happening on the ground has been implementing this. You can't spend half a day driving through the West Bank without seeing it. It's a little harder to drive through Gaza, because it's usually closed off, but essentially the same thing is happening there.

And the situation is extremely serious. Right through the occupation from 1967 to 1993, Israel was making sure – and again, when I say Israel, I mean the United States – was making sure that there would be no development in the occupied territories. So, right after 1993, when Israeli journalists who had covered the territories were finally able to go to Jordan, they were shocked by what they saw and they wrote about it in the Hebrew press. Jordan is a poor country, and Israel is a rich country. Before the 1967 war, the populations in Jordan and the Palestinian populations were pretty comparable, in fact, there was more development in the West Bank. By 1993, it was totally different. In the poorer country Jordan, there were agricultural development, universities, schools, roads, health services, all sorts of things. In the West Bank there was essentially nothing. The people could survive by remittances from abroad, or by doing dirty work in Israel, but no development was allowed, and that was very shocking to Israeli reporters, and it is also backed up in the statistics. The most important work on this topic, if you want to learn about it, is by Sara Roy, a researcher at Harvard who has lived in the Gaza Strip and done the basic scholarly work on it. Just to give you a couple of her figures, current ones, in 1993 electric power usage in the West Bank and Gaza was two-thirds that of Egypt, half that of Jordan – and those are poorer countries, remember. Israel is a rich country. Sanitation in housing in the West Bank and Gaza was about 25 percent, 50 percent in Egypt, and 100 percent in Jordan, and the figures run through that way. GDP per capita, and consumption per capita declined further after 1993. GDP per capita, and consumption per capita have dropped, according to her, about 15 per cent in the West Bank and Gaza since 1993 – that's even with large foreign assistance pouring in, from Europe, mostly.

It's gotten worse in other respects. Up until 1993, the US and Israel permitted humanitarian aid to come into the territories. UN humanitarian aid was permitted into the West Bank and Gaza. In 1993, that was restricted. This is part of the peace process. After Oslo, heavy customs duties were imposed, lots of other restrictions were imposed, you know various kinds of harassment. Now, it's blocked. Right now, humanitarian aid is blocked. The UN is protesting, but it doesn't matter. If the UN protests the blocking of humanitarian aid, and it doesn't register here, it doesn't matter. And it doesn't register here because it's not reported. So they can say, yeah, the Israelis are stopping humanitarian aid from coming in, and people are starving, and so on, but what does it matter as long as people in the United States don't know about it. They can know in the Middle East, they can know in Europe, but it makes no difference. These are our choices again.

For the Palestinians themselves, they are under a dual repression, very much like the Bantustans again, the repression of Israel and the United States, and then the repression of the local mercenaries who do the work for the foreigner, and enrich themselves. It's again a standard, colonial pattern. Anyone who has ever taken a look at the Third World sees it.

As for the goals of Oslo, they were stated very neatly by one of the leading Israeli doves, who was the Minister of Security in the Barak Government, and a temporary foreign minister, known as an academic dove, Shlomo Ben-Ami. In an academic book, 1998, so before he got into the government, he described the goals of Oslo as to impose what he called a permanent neo-colonialist dependency in the West Bank and Gaza. And that's pretty much accurate, that's what the US has been aiming for through the peace process – period.

As for the population, it's kind of hard to improve on a description by Moshe Dayan about 30 years ago. He was in the Labour Party, and among the Labour Party leaders. He was one of those most noted for his sympathetic attitude towards Palestinians, and also his realism. And he described what Israeli policy ought to be, US policy as well. He said the Palestinians should live like dogs and whoever wishes may leave, and we'll see where this leads. Reasonable policy, and that's US policy as well, and it will continue that way as long as we agree to permit it.

Reaping the Whirlwind
The Taliban Movement in Afghanistan
Michael Griffin

'Michael Griffin has reached a better understanding of the Taliban than I have come across anywhere else. This is a highly intelligent account of one of the most interesting and disturbing political movements in the world ... Essential reading.'
John Simpson, BBC

Hb • £19.99 • 0 7453 1274 8

Propaganda and the Public Mind
Conversations with David Barsamian
Noam Chomsky

World renowned dissident Noam Chomsky examines the institutions that shape the public mind in the service of power and profit.

Pb • £10.99 • 0 7453 1788 X

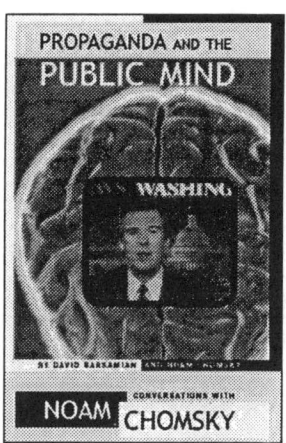

Children of Other Worlds
Exploitation in the Global Market
Jeremy Seabrook

'Seabrook is one of England's most imaginative and creative writers' **The Guardian**

An eye-opening look at the effect of the consumer market on children in the East and West.

Pb • £10.99 • 0 7453 1391 4

PLUTO PRESS

Independent Progressive Publishing
www.plutobooks.com

Nuclear Warfare Revisited

Ken Coates

Ken Coates is the editor of The Spokesman and Chairman of the Bertrand Russell Peace Foundation.

For a very long time, the development of nuclear weapons (and associated military technology), was inextricably related to the progress of the Cold War. From 1945 onwards, fear of Communism ranged the United States and its European allies into what quickly became the North Atlantic Treaty Organisation. An Eastern Alliance, the Warsaw Treaty Organisation, emerged shortly afterwards. The balance of power became more and more dependent on military strength, and immense efforts were put into the refinement of nuclear weapons. The resultant arms race became ever more expensive as destructive capacity became ever more unimaginable. In the West fear of Communism not only stimulated military co-ordination: for a time, it also promoted economic co-operation, and the ascendancy thoughout the West of what is now thought of as the Keynesian world order. These were to be the years of a social welfare consensus in Western Europe, and of the emerging Common Market. Public planning and governmental intervention prospered in the West European economy as never before. Undoubtedly leaders such as Jean Monnet drew support from the business communities with which they were working, on the supposition that their policies would help to fortify the institutions of liberal democracy in the West. Were not Stalin's tanks massed along the newly defined Eastern border? And were not the Communist Parties in Italy and France able to count their votes in many millions?

But if the phobias of the time guaranteed a long period of full employment and relative prosperity, they also launched frenetic military competition. Ultimately the welfare consensus began to wear off: but the military confrontation proved more enduring.

Those who had worked on the development of the bomb in the United States had not expected that it should be tried out on cities without prior warning. They had presumed that a public test of its powers might be made at sea, or in some unpopulated area. In fact, the decision to bomb Hiroshima and Nagasaki seems to have had little to do with military exigencies in the war with Japan, which was already drawing to a close. The presumption of many, politicians and scholars alike, is that the first nuclear bombardment took place in answer to the felt need of the American leadership to send a chilling message to the Soviet Union.

In a very short time, Stalin showed that he had understood, and the Russians detonated their own bomb four years after the Hiroshima explosion. The Soviet hydrogen bomb followed inexorably, just as had the American fusion device.[1] The nuclear race was on. Soon after there opened the race to perfect intercontinental and other rockets, which might deliver the new weapons.

This contest was precisely encapsulated in the metaphor which Bertrand Russell presented to describe it:

> 'Since the nuclear stalemate became apparent, the Governments of East and West have adopted the policy which Mr. Dulles calls 'brinkmanship'. This is a policy adapted from a sport which, I am told, is practised by some youthful degenerates. This sport is called 'Chicken!'. It is played by choosing a long straight road with a white line down the middle and starting two very fast cars towards each other from opposite ends. Each car is expected to keep the wheels of one side on the white line. As they approach each other, mutual destruction becomes more and more imminent. If one of them swerves from the white line before the other, the other, as he passes, shouts 'Chicken!', and the one who has swerved becomes an object of contempt. As played by irresponsible boys, this game is considered decadent and immoral, though only the lives of the players are risked. But when the game is played by eminent statesmen, who risk not only their own lives but those of many hundreds of millions of human beings, it is thought on both sides that the statesmen on one side are displaying a high degree of wisdom and courage, and only the statesmen on the other side are reprehensible. This, of course, is absurd. Both are to blame for playing such an incredibly dangerous game. The game may be played without misfortune a few times, but sooner or later it will come to be felt that loss of face is more dreadful than nuclear annihilation. The moment will come when neither side can face the derisive cry of 'Chicken!' from the other side. When that moment is come, the statesmen of both sides will plunge the world into destruction.'[2]

But apt though it was in the beginning, the game of 'Chicken!' was soon to become a most inadequate guide to the state of the nuclear threat as it extended into wider areas. The polarisation of world conflict was not to remain absolute. New nuclear powers continuously arrived. At first, people in the grip of the Cold War mentality perceived the French and British bombs as if they were at the service of the overarching Western alliance. The British bombs may have been, but the French were something different. Later the Chinese bomb was also mythically assimilated to the Russian armoury. But in truth the nuclear potential divided allies, as well as cementing enmities: the French bomb was manufactured as a result of an intense political argument about the autonomy of France within the Western alliance system: and the birth of the Chinese nuclear capacity was engendered in a ferocious dispute with China's Russian ally. The growth of Chinese nuclear armaments was simultaneously the eruption of the

Sino-Soviet dispute, which was in due time to generate actual military exchanges, and to cause the Chinese to 'dig deep and store grain' by constructing vast labyrinths of nuclear shelters under their main cities, in preparation for Soviet nuclear attacks.

So rooted had the Cold War mentality become by this time, that senior American Intelligence officers went to considerable lengths to persuade the United States Government and its allies that the quarrel between Russia and China was a mock-battle, got up especially in order to mislead the West, as part of an extremely subtle campaign of world domination. The most eminent proponent of the notion that the Sino-Soviet conflict was an elaborate deception was James Angleton of the CIA, who was much influenced by a Soviet defector called Anatoli Golytsin. The split, he said, was

> 'simply a clever ruse to tempt the United States into commitments and aid to China, which would then be used to weaken and exploit the United States.'

Angleton's suspicions were apparently indulged by Morris Oldfield of MI6, who also refused to believe those of his own specialists who confirmed the reality of the split.[3]

But in reality it was the repeated specific American nuclear threats against China which had convinced the Chinese Government that it needed its own nuclear weapons in order to guarantee its continued independence. Relentless and systematic pressure were undoubtedly a key feature of America's China policy.

This first became public knowledge on the 30th November 1950, during the Korean War, when President Truman called a press conference to announce that he was considering a nuclear bombardment of China. The resultant outcry persuaded Clement Attlee to fly at once to Washington, in order to dissuade the Americans. But after the departure of Truman, the same thought recurred. President Eisenhower told us in his memoirs:

> 'In order to compel the Chinese Communists to accede to an armistice, it was obvious that if we were to go over to a major offensive the war would have to be expanded outside of Korea – with strikes against the supporting Chinese airforce in Manchuria, a blockade of the Chinese coast and similar measures . . . Finally, to keep the attack from becoming overtly costly, it was clear that we would have to use atomic weapons . . . we dropped the word, discreetly, of our intention.'[4]

So the Korean War concluded in the truce at Panmunjon in 1953.

Subsequently Sherman Adams, the White House Chief of Staff, gave his view of these events.

> 'Talking one day with Eisenhower about the events that led up finally to the truce in Korea, I asked him what it was that brought the Communists into line. "Danger of an atomic war", he said without hesitation. "We told them we could not hold a limited war any longer if the Communists welched on any truce. They didn't want a full-scale war or an atomic attack".'[5]

The tensions created in the Korean War were not to die away with the cessation of that conflict. There remained a strong American engagement in the continuing conflict between the two Chinas: mainland China and Taiwan. After the Communist victory in 1949, the United States, and for a long time some of its allies, recognised the exiled government of Chiang Kai-Shek, which established itself in the island of Taiwan, as the legitimate authority in all China. Taiwan occupied the Chinese seat in the Security Council of the United Nations. More American threats, lacking nothing in explicitness, were evoked by the ensuing disputes between China and Taiwan, concerning the Tachen Islands in 1954, and the Islands of Quemoy and Matsu in 1955 and again in 1958. Chiang Kai-Shek was using these Islands for the continued molestation of Chinese shipping, and as jumping off grounds for hit and run raids on the mainland. The Americans confirmed their support for Chiang at each point in this stand off, with direct nuclear warnings. Of course, nuclear confrontation can involve generalised non-specific threats, such as visible deployments or warning manoeuvres. But these threats were direct, anything but hints. In the end, Eisenhower sent the 7th Fleet to the Taiwan Straits, and announced that the United States Air Force had, in readiness for any eventuality, been equipped with nuclear missiles during the Quemoy crisis. This mobilisation cost a billion dollars. Small wonder that the Chinese Communists turned to their Russian allies with a request for countervailing power.

However, the Soviet leaders were nervous about devolving nuclear weapons into the control of their largest ally. They sensed that they might court total destruction themselves if they yielded the nuclear initiative to a proxy.

Even so, on the 15th October 1957, a secret agreement was reached by which the Russians undertook to provide the Chinese with 'a sample of an atomic bomb and technical data concerning its manufacture'. But after the later Quemoy crisis there were second thoughts about this issue, because the Soviet Government believed (and the historian Roy Medvedev tends to think they were right[6]) that the Chinese were provoking an incident for reasons of their own. From this distance, in the absence of inside information, it is quite impossible to provide categorical proof either way: but it does appear perfectly clear that Chiang Kai-Shek was himself an adept provocateur and had a permanent interest in maintaining the highest level of tension between People's China and his American backers. Quemoy was not an innocent desert island, but an advanced and active military base, and the Chinese bombardment of it was arguably a reasonable form of self-protection.

This indeed, whatever he thought privately, was the public assumption of Khrushchev in his message to Eisenhower on 8th September 1958. If we are to regard Khrushchev's memoirs as authentic, they show that in fact he went a great deal further than this.

'We were all in favour of Mao Tse-Tung's liquidating these two islands as potential jumping off points' he wrote.[7]

Chiang, he thought, was hoping to recover possession of the mainland and the Americans were 'egging him on'. Indeed, Khrushchev expresses his impatience because the Chinese were not more resolute in pressing their offensive. 'You can imagine our surprise' he said, 'when the balance tipped in favour of Mao Tse-Tung ...' but 'they suddenly halted their offensive. As a result the whole operation came to nothing'.

In any case, what is not in dispute is that the Chinese later asserted publicly that after the Quemoy face-off, on 20th June 1959, the Russians unilaterally 'tore up' their 1957 promise. It is also beyond doubt that thereafter Moscow cut off all direct nuclear assistance to Beijing. Khrushchev indeed was attempting to promote the idea of an Asian nuclear-free zone in his discussions with the Americans, even though the Chinese were not parties to this proposal.

All the public polemics between Russia and China on ideological questions, including the acrimonious debate on the question of the alleged 'inevitability' of war, followed these events. Not one of the main doctrinal quarrels preceded them. There were undoubtedly gross excesses in the polemic war which became known as the Sino-Soviet dispute. As often happens, this dispute appears to have gained a momentum of its own. However, it did not fall out of the blue, and its aggravation was to a very considerable degree influenced by specific events, which were far from being simply matters of doctrine.

In 1963 the Cold War stand-off between the United States and the Soviet Union came to a head in the October crisis in Cuba. Khrushchev had agreed to deploy intermediate range nuclear missiles in Cuba, to deter any repetition of the 1961 Bay of Pigs invasion. President Kennedy insisted on the withdrawal of all such missiles, and imposed a naval blockade to prevent the importation of arms to Cuba. The Cubans appealed to the Russians not to give way, and it became clear that a Soviet fleet of ships, some of which carried arms, was approaching Cuba. An armada awaited them. Here was the chicken game fully operational, on the high seas. In the event it was Khrushchev who swerved, and the world survived. But the Soviet Government drew the conclusion that the avoidance of any similar climb down required that it should embark upon a superhuman programme to construct overwhelming nuclear force. Cuba frightened the civilised world, but escalated the Cold War arms race beyond anyone's imagination. However, if most of the world saw the Cuba crisis as a momentary reprieve, and accepted it with relief, in China it looked quite different. Now it was evident that the Russian leadership would not risk the destruction of Russia in order to defend its allies.

The Chinese thenceforward entered on a policy of self-reliance, and exploded their own atomic bomb in October 1964. Within the short space of three years they had progressed to the point where they were able to detonate a thermo-nuclear explosion on 17th June 1967. Delivery systems of such weapons were very much more difficult to perfect. A large part of the technical problem in preparing a nuclear explosion inheres in the difficulty involved in refining a sufficient quantity of fissionable material. This is much easier to do if there exists an expendable labour force who are allowed to die of radiation poisoning, and thus enable development to dispense with the need for complex robotic handling techniques. It appears very possible that the speedy growth of Soviet nuclear technology may well have initially depended on such a grizzly involvement of human forces. The Chinese successes might not have been so costly in human terms, because the first Chinese bomb, according to American monitors who checked on the results of its explosion, was not a simple plutonium device but a more sophisticated one using a rare uranium isotope.

Be that as it may, for the Soviet leaders, Chinese progress in nuclear armament was doubly upsetting. Even though the Chinese bomb was for a long time lacking in any adequate delivery mechanism, these leaders saw the writing on the wall.

Part of the writing contained a message of simple opportunism. Henceforth nuclear proliferation offered a potential new danger, and the Americans were probably already influenced by this when they moved towards the conclusion of a Test Ban Treaty with the Russians in 1963. The Chinese called this 'a big fraud'. The following year, Averell Harriman asked Khrushchev what Russia would do if Washington decided to eliminate Chinese nuclear sites[8]. This was the first time such a question arose between great nuclear powers: but it would not be the last. Very soon it was Soviet diplomats who were exploring American responses to the question, 'How would you react if we were to launch a pre-emptive attack?' The Russians never nuked the Chinese atomic installations: but ferocious squabbles turned into physical battles in a protracted border conflict, which raised tension to a very high level.

This was not reduced by events in Czechoslovakia, where the evolution of 'socialism with a human face' triggered a full-scale intervention by the Soviet Union and its allies in the Warsaw Treaty, in 1968, shortly before the Czechoslovak Communists were scheduling their 14th Party Congress. The Chinese were by now involved in a frenetic political and ideological squabble with the Soviet leaders, and were themselves preparing for their 9th Congress in April 1969. The notions of limited sovereignty which were clearly implied by the invasion of Czechoslovakia, and the installation of a puppet Government, were anything but acceptable to the Chinese. But of course, the sovereignty of China was a more difficult quality to limit than was that of Czechoslovakia.

Whilst the Sino-Soviet confrontation intensified, on the 11th September 1969, Premier Chou En-Lai met with Premier Kosygin in Beijing. It is difficult to disentangle the knot of threads which had been tied before this meeting, but it appears clear that the Russians were threatening a surgical strike against Chinese nuclear installations, and that Chou En-Lai insisted that any such strike would bring about all-out war. But the Soviet threat 'worked', in that negotiations between the two Communist powers resumed. However, the underlying situation was clearly not resolved, but greatly aggravated. Then began the feverish campaign in China to construct nuclear shelters in every major city. Immense labyrinths were dug beneath Beijing and other major towns.

All this remarkable history is relevant, because it reveals how far the chicken game had extended itself into an inconceivable map of suicidal potential, in which a variety of vehicles could approach each other on different axes, making collisions completely unpredictable, and thus grossly jeopardising any possible future.

The calculations which the Russians had to make were superficially simple. Their chicken vehicle was very powerful, and the Chinese opponent was very frail. A collision would probably entail small damage to Russia, but dreadful destruction to China. But all the time there was the larger game, in which the mighty American vehicle might unleash itself against the Russians. How would the Americans respond to a bombardment of China? Of course, the Chinese perceived this dimension of the problem, which is why we saw in short order, the meeting between President Nixon and Mao Tse-Tung, and the American declaration that they 'would not be indifferent to a Soviet attack on China'.

Already, other games of chicken were beginning to shape up. Would the Chinese intervene in a conflict between Pakistan and India, to protect their Pakistan allies? If they did, would the Russians seize the opportunity to defend their Indian allies by a strike on China?

All this complexity was indeed faced down, and by some sort of miracle, no nuclear exchanges took place.

But, if we jump forward to examine the situation a quarter of a century later, we can begin to intuit a very real new danger.

The game of chicken, so naturally an analogy to Russell at the time when the Cold War dominated international relations, was, we can now see, in fact already beginning to break apart when his vital little book was first published. Within a decade, to all intents and purposes, it had gone. Even so, the Cold War dominated the political imagination. But all the while, nuclear proliferation sped ahead. The development of the Israeli bomb brought a new dimension into the balance of power, and terror, in the Middle East. Nuclear research hastened ahead in India and Pakistan. The list of countries anticipated to be on the brink of nuclear testing extended itself in the most daunting way. Dark talk of Islamic bombs became more and more noisy. But in 1963 President Kennedy had anticipated that up to twenty countries would have nuclear weapons by 1975. This did not happen. The Non-Proliferation Treaty, which came into force in 1970, soon gathered more than 150 adherents, and has now enrolled 187. But the failure of the five main nuclear powers to show any willingness to meet the Treaty commitment to negotiate about their own nuclear disarmament was to bring continuous disruptive pressures to bear.[9] A succession of review conferences has understandably found it more and more difficult to renew the Treaty, in this context.

The alleged end of the Cold War began by denuclearising some parts of the former Soviet Union. But this process was accompanied by a deceptive movement in alleged 'deterrence' doctrine. Far from leading to mutual disarmament it saw a continuous extension of American power, ultimately matched by a deterioration in the Russian response, which became more, not less nuclear with the abandonment of the long-standing commitment to 'no first use'.

Because of the grip of the Cold War on all our thinking, the end of bipolar confrontation was assumed to mean a radical new departure in terms of nuclear doctrine. After all, history had ended, had it not? Opponents of American hegemony called for a multipolar world. In terms of the diffusion of political power and space for democratic opposition, this had much to be said for it. But in terms of nuclear chicken, it was clearly a most difficult area. Serial confrontations could easily become entangled, repeating the experience of the Russian, Chinese and American stand-offs at the end of the 1960s, and aggravating them with the 'progress' in nuclear armaments of India, or Pakistan, or Iran, or a host of other territories.

In 1995, Michael Mandelbaum, the Director of the American Project on East-West Relations in Washington, cast a cold eye over the immediate future when he offered us 'Lessons of the Next Nuclear War'[10]. Three different categories of states were now candidates for nuclear armaments, he told us. The first group were those whose acquisition of nuclear weapons would impact most strongly on international policies.

> 'They are the allies. Germany and Japan forswore nuclear weapons during the Cold War because they received security guarantees from the United States. Whether they continue as non-nuclear states depends on whether those guarantees continue.'

To be more accurate we might add that the continuity of the American 'umbrella' may not be all that is required. If that umbrella takes the form, now proposed, of the National Missile Defence, more widely known as 'Son of Star Wars', it may provoke such instability in the relations between these allies and, say Russia or China, as to hasten them towards making the very decision to go independently nuclear, which it is Mr. Mandelbaum's ardent desire to avoid.

The most likely form of German proliferation would follow the development of a European 'deterrent' in the course of closer military integration within the European Union. This might be 'justified' with reference to the resolutions of the Western European Union, a defence organ with a sternly nuclear deterrent philosophy. But however it was presented, proliferation within the Atlantic Alliance would pose all the risks we saw earlier in the steady deterioration of the Sino-Soviet alliance once both parties embarked on becoming nuclear powers. The bomb offers an even more powerful menace to allies than it does to antagonists.[11]

Leaving aside the allies, the second group of would-be nuclear powers are what Mandelbaum calls the 'orphans'.

> 'They feel seriously threatened but lack the nuclear protection the allies have enjoyed. None has become a full-fledged nuclear power but each is close. The orphans, particularly Pakistan, Israel and Ukraine, are the objects of a different American policy – diplomatic efforts to end the conflicts that have made nuclear armaments attractive to them.'

But America's diplomatic efforts are not disinterested, and follow the perceived interests of the American Government. This interest has been bluntly stated, in

1997, in respect of Ukraine, by Zbigniew Brzezinski in his blueprint for American policy, **The Grand Chessboard**[12]. It sees American power as dependent on the establishment and maintenance of hegemony over Ukraine, which is defined as part of the critical core or 'geopolitical pivot' of 'American primacy'. Whether in fact this is to become the case or not, it is perfectly clear that at present Ukraine has been quite incapable of ceasing to be part of the old Soviet economy however many efforts it has made. This is one orphan which is likely to generate continual insecurity, whilst the other two which are named by Mandelbaum are even more obviously centres of volatility. Both, incidentally, can now be seen to be very much further advanced in nuclear capacity than Mandelbaum apparently thought as recently as 1995.

Mandelbaum's third category are the rogues, notably Iraq and North Korea.

> 'The prevention of proliferation may ultimately require destroying those states' nuclear programmes by force'.

Here again, says Mandelbaum, 'the chief responsibility will fall to the United States'. But if more American raids are to be unleashed, on territories which are outside the imperium of the world's pre-eminent superpower, the one certain outcome will be to engender greater nervousness among the 'allies', and greater instability among the 'orphans'.

Is it thinkable that comprehensive nuclear disarmament might come to seem preferable to this bizarre evolution? Doubtless hoping to encourage the signatories of the Non-Proliferation Treaty to stand by their earlier commitments, the five nuclear powers did, at the beginning of the new Millennium, find it necessary to conclude an agreement jointly to move towards nuclear disarmament, within this framework of the Non-Proliferation Treaty.[13] Before we greet this joint resolution with too much enthusiasm, we are bound to note that it has no timetable, no fixed staging points, and no means of enforcement.[14] But it does appear at a moment when it was necessary to dissuade new powers from beginning the construction of nuclear weapons.

Mandelbaum's dismal analysis presumes no surge towards disarmament. On the contrary, it seems to anticipate certain moves to proliferation:

> 'The United States has at least one reason to welcome German and Japanese nuclear weapons. They would relieve Americans of defending two countries sufficiently wealthy and powerful to defend themselves and separated from North America by large oceans.'

However, even if all this was an advantage to the American defence appropriations it would

> 'cause more than a ripple in international politics: it would make waves. The change would usher in a multipolar nuclear order, which would supplant the more or less bipolar arrangement of the Cold War. A multipolar order would by some reckonings make the world more dangerous – less stable, less certain and less easily managed. In multipolar systems, none of the great powers can ever be certain who will side with whom.'

Here we reach the nub of the question. For the United States, it is not a good idea to render the world 'less easily managed'. But there is another way to manage the world, which does not require the concentration of nuclear force. It requires better behaviour by those with power, which might encourage better behaviour to become more widespread.

In this respect, Bertrand Russell's little book *Common Sense and Nuclear Warfare* has stood the test of time. We have lived through the Cold War, and survived the extension of the famous chicken game into ever more dangerous, and ever more baroque, permutations. Now, it seems, we have lived through the post-Cold War, and squandered every opportunity for orderly progress towards comprehensive disarmament and the development of a genuinely new world order. The bombardment of Yugoslavia by Nato, which kicked away the veto in the UN Security Council, the last surviving constitutional safeguard for the interests of Russia and China as minority participants in international relations, was a bridge too far for the Russian political classes.

Economically enfeebled, and thus greatly disadvantaged in conventional military forces, the Russians had seen Nato advancing closer and closer to their borders, and establishing joint military exercises with states which formerly belonged to the Soviet Union. Now, with the nullification of the UN Charter, the last international safeguard of the post-war settlement, they embarked upon policies which clearly marked the beginning of a third phase in the nuclear age.

All through the Cold War, Russian leaders had insisted upon a doctrine of 'no first use' of nuclear weapons. The Americans declined to embrace this doctrine on the grounds that the Russians had superior conventional forces, and that they could therefore offer no guarantee that an armed attack of any kind might not be rebuffed by nuclear strikes. But now the Russian conventional forces are the weaker, in a context in which guerrilla insurgencies are already testing their powers. So we have arrived at the Putin doctrine, which specifically rescinds no first use. At the same time, as we have seen, the National Missile Defence, a refinement of the Strategic Defence Initiative once pursued by President Reagan, is again threatening to disrupt, even reverse, progress towards further specific agreements on East-West nuclear disarmament. Clearly the Russians cannot match those American technologies which purport to enable space-based missiles to destroy attacking salvos from wherever they may come. (The Americans themselves are not finding it easy.) So we must expect that the Russians will raise their game elsewhere.

Common sense is nowhere to be seen in this stand-off, which may now generate even more widespread proliferation, and even more random oppositions between the powers. Those who thought Russell's warnings were no longer relevant are clearly, sadly, mistaken. It is time to grease up the walking boots, and refurbish the banners, because the only rational response to this nightmare of opposing weapons is, as it was, nuclear disarmament.

Footnotes

1 See the three articles by Zhores Medvedev on the development of nuclear weapons in the USSR, in **The Spokesman**, Nos 67, 68 and 69, 1999/2000.
2 **Common Sense and Nuclear Warfare**, p30.
3 This episode came to light during the controversy about **Spy Catcher**, the autobiography of Peter Wright, one-time Assistant Director of MI5. The memoirs of other spies are carefully dissected by Stephen Dorril, in **MI6 – Fifty Years of Special Operations**, Fourth Estate, London, pp. 713 et seq.
4 Dwight D. Eisenhower: **Mandate for Change**, Vol. 1, New York, Doubleday, pp. 178-81.
5 Cited by Daniel Ellsberg: Call to Mutiny, in **Endpapers One**, Spokesman, Nottingham, 1981, p.20.
6 Roy Medvedev: **China and the Superpowers**, Oxford, Blackwell, 1986.
7 Nikita Khrushchev: **Khrushchev Remembers**, London, Deutsch, 1974, page 262. Strictly speaking, there is not any question about the authenticity of Khrushchev's memoirs. In fact, the full original transcript of the tapes of these memoirs have been published in Moscow in 1999 in four huge volumes of approximately one thousand pages each. Questions of authenticity arise for two reasons. First, Khrushchev's tapes were dictated from memory, since he was deprived of access to official papers. So these volumes represent a formidable power of recall, even though it is inevitable that sometimes the author's memory should fail him. Secondly, the editing of this vast memoir was a gargantuan task, brilliantly performed, since the memoirs are certainly most readable. But the process of editing, at a distance from the author, and from any primary sources, must necessarily pose difficulties.

    It is interesting that Khrushchev embarked on this huge project, after a suggestion from Bertrand Russell.
8 Franz Schurmann: **The Logic of World Power**, New York, Pantheon, 1974, p 55.
9 Article VI of the Treaty committed the nuclear powers to 'pursue negotiations in good faith . . . under strict and effective international control'.
10 Michael Mandelbaum: 'Lessons of the Next Nuclear War', **Foreign Affairs**, March / April 1995.
11 Mr. Mandelbaum's nightmare appeared to be approaching reality when, on July 13th 2000, the **Morning Star** reported:

> 'Peace campaigners slammed a call by French Foreign Minister Hubert Vedrine for a single nuclear weapon for the European Union yesterday as 'backdoor nuclear proliferation'.
> Mr. Vedrine claimed that nuclear weapons were 'an extreme guarantee of survival. 'To assure the credibility of dissuasion, there is a need for a single dissuader.
> "Peace is guaranteed by this mechanism. To transfer this position to a European level there is a need that the dissuader be credible and speak in the name of a single European people", he said.'

Upon checking, this story was found to be based on a Reuter's report of July 12th, which said:

> 'The French Foreign Minister Hubert Vedrine said in an interview published on Wednesday that Europe some day may need a single nuclear power to speak as a deterrent force for the whole continent.'

However, the Reuter report went on to say that Vedrine thought it too early to say what role France and Britain, the European Union's only nuclear powers, would have in a

European deterrent.

Reference to the published version of this interview in **La Repubblica**, shows that even this version of Vedrine's remarks is somewhat misleading. Vedrine was responding to a direct question from the newspaper. Germany had renounced the Mark, and thus their monetary sovereignty. But on the military plane France had not renounced its nuclear weapons, which would have been an equivalent sacrifice to the German monetary gesture. Vedrine's response was 'That is a false symmetry'. He had then gone on to defend the French deterrent, and to argue that a European deterrent would not be possible until European Union had reached the stage in which one could speak of a single European people. 'Today it is not like that'.

That such questions naturally occur to an Italian journalist shows that this idea is current. But Vedrine's answer shows that it is not yet about to become reality. All this will depend on the development of relations between Europe and the United States. It will be a brave person who will insist that these relationships will always continue as they have been.

12 Zbigniew Brzezinski: **The Grand Chessboard**, Basic Books, 1997.
13 The press release of 22nd May 2000 reported that the Non-Proliferation Review Conference 'after marathon last-minute negotiations' had finally agreed on the immediate disarmament priorities for the international community, as the 2000 Review Conference of Parties to Treaty on Non-Proliferation of Nuclear Weapons (NPT) concluded its four-week session early Saturday evening.

Capping a 15-year effort to produce a consensus outcome, the 155 NPT States parties present, out of a total of 187, agreed that there should be 'an unequivocal undertaking by the nuclear-weapon States to accomplish the total elimination of their nuclear arsenals'.
14 All these missing features could be rectified, but this is unlikely to happen in the absence of massive public agitation and protest.

My grateful acknowledgements to Michael Barratt Brown, George Farebrother, Bruce Kent, Zhores Medvedev, Eileen Noakes, Dhirendra Sharma and Tony Simpson for their helpful comments on the first draft of this paper.

The Militarist Camp in the United States

Immanuel Wallerstein

Immanuel Wallerstein is Director of the Fernand Braudel Center, Binghampton University, State University of New York.

George W. Bush has made it quite clear, quite rapidly, that his Administration will govern the United States as far to the right as it politically can. How far can it? To answer that, it is not enough to look at the balance of political forces between the Democrats and the Republicans. Most commentators seem to emphasise how closely the two parties are balanced at the moment in the United States Congress. This is the wrong way to look at it. The fact is that this is the first time in forty years and only the second time since 1932 that the Republican Party has controlled the Presidency and both Houses of Congress. Numbers of bills that the Republicans favoured in the last six years and for which they had the votes in Congress were either vetoed by Clinton or were withdrawn in the face of a threatened veto. The Republicans are today in a relatively strong position, despite the closeness of the presidential election and despite the narrow margins they have in the legislature.

The real political question to look at is potential struggles within the Republican Party. Thus far, Bush has been able to hold the factions together, but can this last? Throughout the post-1945 period, there have always been three quite different constituencies that have made up the Republican Party: the economic conservatives, the social conservatives, and the macho militarists. Of course, many individuals are all three, but most persons give priority to one of the three thrusts. And therein lies the problem for the Republicans.

The economic conservatives are mostly businessmen and their cadres plus high-earning professionals. Their priority at the moment is to reduce their tax burden and to resist any effort to force enterprises to internalise their costs (via ecological legislation). With amazing rapidity, Bush has indicated that he will fight very hard for everything this constituency wants. And they seem clearly to be his personal priority. He may not get everything he wants in tax reduction. But he will probably get almost everything he wants in restricting environmental protection, since a large part of what is needed to be done requires the action of the Executive branch of government. He has already repealed a good deal of what Clinton tried to put into effect in the closing days of his Administration. And he has shut the door definitively on the Kyoto Protocol. To the Europeans (and Canadians) who are unanimously very upset, he has said unequivocally that the interests of US businessmen are his first concern.

The social conservatives have played an increasingly important role in Republican politics over the last 25 years, due to the mobilisation of the Christian Coalition. Bush has gone out of his way to make serious gestures to meet their demands. He has reinstated the ban on giving any money to any international organisation that indicates in any way that it favours abortions. He has appointed one of them as the Attorney-General, a key post. And he has in effect promised that his Supreme Court appointments would be ones they would favour. But he may not be able to get those appointments ratified. We shall see. However, in matters of new legislation, he has in effect told the social conservatives that they must do the work themselves to get the bills passed, and that, if they succeed, he promises to sign them. But it seems he is not going to spend too much of his own political ammunition in an effort to achieve these ends.

The joker in the pack is macho militarism. In a few short months, the Bush Administration has managed to take on the entire world. Whereas the Clinton Administration seemed to think that US interests were served by calming down conflicts across the world (to be sure, in ways that the US found comfortable), the Bush people seem almost to be stoking up the conflicts. They have said that a lot more has to be done about Saddam Hussein. They have withdrawn from mediating Israel/Palestine, and have shifted from a covertly pro-Israel position to an overtly pro-Israel, anti-Arafat position, They have flexed their muscles with the Canadians and the West Europeans by telling them in no uncertain terms that the United States will proceed with the new missile defence proposals, and have shown little interest in maintaining the old United States-Russian nuclear treaties, saying they are outdated. They have downgraded the Russians from being a potential ally to being again a potential enemy. They seem to be on the point of giving Taiwan the kind of arms they want and which the Chinese have made clear it is their priority for them not to get. As for easing anything on the Cuba embargo, forget it.

And of course, they seem determined to keep North Korea as an active enemy. This last posture has upset the European Union so much that they have sent a special delegation to North Korea, presumably to see if Europe could supply some of the financial assistance that the United States is clearly no longer ready to negotiate.

Romano Prodi, the President of the European Union Commission, has already accused the United States of failing to act like a 'world leader' because of its narrow nationalist attitudes on the question of global warming. Mr. Bush seems oblivious. In his Press Conference on March 29, there occurred the following extraordinary exchange:

> Question: 'Mr. President, allies of the United States have complained that you haven't consulted them sufficiently on your stance with negotiations with North Korea, Kyoto Treaty, your deteriorating relations elsewhere. If you strictly read the international press, it looks like everyone's mad at us. Mr. President, how do you think that came to be? And what, if anything, do you plan to do about it?'
>
> Answer: 'Well, I get a completely different picture, of course, when I sit down with the world leaders.'
>
> Bush then went on to say on the carbon dioxide issue that 'we will not do anything that harms our economy, because first things first, are the people who live in America. That's my priority.'

Is it really true that Bush is unaware of the fact that everyone is mad at the United States, or does he not care? This is where the macho militarists come in. This group believes that power talks, and that if the United States doesn't act tough, it will lose everything -- its power, its wealth, its centrality in the world-system. They don't want to settle conflicts; they want to win conflicts. And if it requires a little military action here or there, they are ready and eager. The big question is, are the American people eager or even ready? And even more important for Bush, are the businessmen, who are his basic support group and the group to which he owes his loyalty, ready? Because, although military armaments generate a lot of profits (Shaw explained all this wonderfully in Major Barbara), it is also true that unnecessary wars interfere with capitalist profits in many different ways (Schumpeter always argued this). One of the major reasons why Clinton (and before him Bush the father) improved relations with China was the pressure of Republican businessmen, who wanted to invest and trade there. And it was Republican farm interests which pressed Clinton to ease the Cuban embargo. The militarist wing of the Republican Party runs against the grain of the economic conservative wing (or at least a part of it).

So the macho militarists may find arrayed against them not merely those they regard as their enemies (say, China and Russia) and the major United States allies but perhaps some major transnationals and other large US businesses. This may cause Bush to rein in the macho militarists, because if he doesn't they might escalate the provocations. Is Bush strong enough to do this?

Teddy Roosevelt, unabashed spokesman of United States imperialism, advised 'Speak softly and carry a big stick.' The Bush administration is not following this advice. They are speaking quite loudly indeed. But what is the size of their stick?

Missile Defence: Pretext Absurd

Joseph Rotblat

Professor Rotblat, together with the Pugwash Conferences on Science and World Affairs, was awarded the Nobel Peace Prize in 1995.

It may be right that the US ballistic missile defence (BMD) system will be built, even though it is unlikely ever to be 100 per cent effective. But it is wrong, in my opinion, to imply that BMD would enhance world security. On the contrary, it would endanger world security.

The Anti-Ballistic Missile (ABM) Treaty of 1972 will almost certainly be the victim of the decision to proceed with ballistic missile defence, and it is important to remind ourselves of the significance of this treaty. At the time the treaty was negotiated, the US Administration was in favour of it while the Soviet Union was strongly opposed to it. At the Pugwash Conferences we managed to convince our Russian colleagues to persuade their Government that ballistic missile defence would be bound to result in an intensification of the nuclear arms race, because any such system could be saturated by the use of a larger number of missiles, and offensive missiles are much cheaper than defensive ones. Three decades later, and this argument is still valid.

Although the Cold War is over, the mindset on nuclear issues has survived: we still seem to rely on the nuclear deterrent for world security. But if the US were protected by a ballistic missile defence system, Russia and China would have lost their deterrents and be compelled to restore the balance by increasing their nuclear arsenals – a new nuclear arms race. Officially, of course, ballistic missile defence is not intended to defend against Russia or China but against 'rogue states' (or 'states of concern' in current jargon). But this pretext is absurd. Any nuclear attack with ballistic missiles would be suicidal for those states. If such states, or terrorist groups sponsored by them, wanted to injure the US, this could be achieved by cheaper means and with less risk of reprisal.

Anyhow, there is an alternative way to deal with the nuclear threat, whether from rogue states or from overt or covert nuclear states, namely, by the creation of a nuclear-weapon-free world, safeguarded by a robust verification and enforcement regime. The United Kingdom (as well as the United States) is legally committed to the elimination of nuclear weapons. In pursuance of this policy – and for the sake of world peace – the United Kingdom should make an effort to convince the US Administration to abandon the Ballistic Missile Defence project.

TRANSPORT & GENERAL WORKERS' UNION
South East & East Anglia

On International Workers' Day the T&G sends solidarity greetings to trade unionists and their allies the world over.

Every worker a member, every member an organiser!

Eddie McDermott
Regional Secretary

Patsy Payne
Regional Chair

(p) **020 8800 4281**   (f) **020 8802 8388**
(e-mail) **emcdermott@tgwu.org.uk**

Satellite Killers and Space Dominance

Compiled by Bob Aldridge

Bob Aldridge works at the Pacific Life Research Centre. He is the author of First Strike: The Pentagon's Strategy for Nuclear War.

'...the Department of Defence must have the appropriate capabilities to deny when necessary an adversary's use of space systems to support hostile military forces.'
— William S. Cohen, former US Secretary of Defence[1]

Anti-Satellite (ASAT) warfare is an important element in a United States first-strike capability. If, simultaneously with or slightly before launching Trident and other missiles to destroy an opponent's missiles in their silos, the United States could knock out the opponent's communications and early warning satellites, it would delay getting the fire command to the opponent's missiles before they are destroyed. Anti-Satellite warfare would probably be the first move in a United States first strike.

It is actually easier to destroy a satellite in a known and tracked orbit than to instantaneously detect, target and destroy a ballistic missile out of the blue. Furthermore, satellites do not presently have defences such as decoys and other types of spoofing. Since missiles and satellites entered the modern age, schemes to destroy both of them have been closely interwoven. Ballistic missile defence and anti-satellite programmes, ostensibly separated and autonomous, have supplemented and reinforced each other for decades. The National Missile Defence, and possibly the upper tier Tactical Missile Defence, interceptors would be more effective against low-orbit satellites than they would against missiles. That is because the location of satellites is known for any point in time and there are no counter-measures. The airborne laser and the space-based laser would also be much more effective against satellites where they only shoot through the void of space, as opposed to shooting down into the atmosphere at missiles in their boost phase. The atmosphere tends to spread the laser beam (called blooming) so it is diffused and cannot be concentrated on a vital spot. Lasers might also be effective against higher satellites in geosynchronous orbit. Likewise, the early warning and X-band radars being developed for ballistic missile defence will have inherent space-tracking capabilities.

Converted inter-continental ballistic missiles or submarine-launched ballistic missiles would make good booster rockets for hit-to-kill vehicles against satellites. The hit-to-kill technology has already been tried against satellites. The main obstacle to anti-satellite development is explained by Major Kurt Stevens of the Air Force Space Command's planning directorate: 'The bottom line is that you've got to develop the public and congressional support that understands that there is a need for an ASAT.'[2] Air Force officials acknowledge that politics, not technology, is the main obstacle to anti-satellite development. Meanwhile United States anti-satellite activities quietly profit from ballistic missile defence developments.

A short history

It wasn't long after the Soviets put Sputnik in orbit that the United States started pursuing anti-satellite technologies. In 1959 a Bold Orion rocket was launched from a B-47 bomber to intercept the Explorer-6 satellite over Cape Canaveral.

Anti-satellite studies were taking place from 1960 to 1962. They included using a microwave (MASER) beam to destroy satellites, blinding satellites with paint to cover their optical window, and deploying a cloud of metal pellets in a satellite's path. Programmes specific to this study were the Satellite Interceptor (SAINT), the Manned Orbital Laboratory (MOL), and the Ballistic Missile Boost Intercept (BAMBI). All three branches of the military got into the act. It should be noted that, since there is no blast effect in space, satellites can only be destroyed if they are hit by a physical object of high-energy radiation.

From May 1963 until January 1966 the Army conducted a project at Kwajalein Atoll called 'Project Mudflap.' At least eight Nike-Zeus anti-ballistic missile interceptors were fired with nuclear warheads. The first ground-launched intercept occurred on 23 May 1963 when an Agena-D spacecraft was hit in orbit. There was believed to be an operational system on Kwajalein Atoll until 1968.

The Navy project was called 'Early Spring.' It used a modified Polaris submarine-launched ballistic missile to scatter metal pellets in a satellite's orbit.

Johnston Island in the Pacific was the scene of the Air Force's 'Project 437 Thor.' At least sixteen 'thrust augmented' Thor rockets were launched with a manoeuvering second stage and nuclear warheads. This system was believed to have been operational until 1975 and could reach satellites up to 800 miles altitude over a radius of 1,700 miles. About this time it was discovered that nuclear explosions in space created an electro-magnetic pulse (EMP) that destroyed our own satellites and other electronics hundreds of miles away.

During the 1980s anti-satellite activities went along parallel with Ronald Reagan's Star Wars charade. In 1981 the Air Force was given the go-ahead for a first generation anti-satellite programme. This air-launched anti-satellite vehicle used a short-range attack missile (SRAM) first stage with a Thiokol Altaire-3 second stage, and had a 900-mile range. It was launched from an F-15 aircraft in a steep climb and pointed at the target. The warhead was a non-nuclear, hit-to-kill vehicle with infrared sensors to see the target and small rocket motors to guide it onto a collision course. The first test on 21 January 1984 did not use a warhead and was only aimed at a point in space. Obviously, it was a success. The second test on 13 November 1984 used the infrared sensors to find the light from a star. It had a cooling line failure. A test of the complete system at an actual target took place on 13 September 1985 against a 345-mile-high Solwind satellite. Two more tests followed in August and September of 1986 against the light from a star – each time a star closer to the horizon.

A total of twelve tests were scheduled with a planned initial operational capability in 1987 for an eventual force of over 100 interceptors. However, when the estimated system cost skyrocketed over tenfold, the Air Force cut the programme back. After technical problems and testing delays compounded the troubles, anti-satellite activities were cancelled by the administration in 1988. Shortly thereafter, Congress banned tests against any object in space unless the Soviets broke their self-imposed moratorium on such tests.[3]

Current anti-satellite interest

There has been no waning in the Pentagon's desire to wage war in space – 'space control,' as it is euphemistically called today. Although anti-satellite activities are not the whole of space warfare, neither are they at the bottom of the list. General Ralph E. Eberhart – commander-in-chief of the North American Aerospace

GLOSSARY

AGIL	*All Gas Iodine Laser.*
ASAT	*Anti-Satellite.*
BAMBI	*Ballistic Missile Boost Intercept.*
BMD	*Ballistic Missile Defence.*
DoD	*Department Of Defence.*
EMP	*Electro-Magnetic Pulse.*
GAO	*General Accounting Office.*
ICBM	*Inter-Continental Ballistic Missile.*
KE-ASAT	*Kinetic Energy ASAT.*
MASER	*Microwave Amplification by Stimulated Emission of Radiation.*
MIRACL	*Mid-InfraRed Advanced Chemical Laser.*
MOL	*Manned Orbital Laboratory.*
NORAD	*North American Aerospace Defence Command.*
SAINT	*Satellite Interceptor.*
SLBM	*Submarine-Launched Ballistic Missile.*
SRAM	*Short-Range Attack Missile.*

Defence Command (NORAD), the United States Space Command, and the Air Force Space Command – said: 'We rely on space for communications, navigation, timing, surveillance, reconnaissance, and weather forecasting.... Not only do we have to use it, we have to be able to defend it and *deny our enemy the use of space if we are at war*.'[4] (Emphasis added) That obviously includes destroying the opponent's satellites.

Numerous recent reports also describe the Pentagon's interest in space warfare and anti-satellite activities. In his 2000 posture statement, Defence Secretary William S. Cohen stated: '...[the Department of Defence] must have the appropriate capabilities to deny when necessary an adversary's use of space systems to support hostile military forces.'[5] A little earlier the Pentagon-commissioned Strategic Studies Group IV similarly stated: 'In order to neutralise – and selectively deny access to – space, the Department of Defence must develop the means to control and destroy space assets (both in space and at ground level), while selectively reconstituting its own capability through multiple sources.'[6]

The Phase II report of the United States Commission on National Security for the 21st Century also addressed the growing importance of space: 'Outer space and cyberspace are the main arteries of the world's evolving information and economic systems.... Through both technical and diplomatic means, the United States needs to guard against the possibility of 'breakout' capabilities in space and cyberspace that would endanger United States survival or critical interests.'[7]

Joint Vision 2020 is the Pentagon's benchmark document for military transformation. In its contribution to that document the United States Space Command stated: 'Indeed, so important are space systems to military operations that it is unrealistic to imagine they will never become targets.... space superiority is emerging as an essential element of battlefield success and future warfare.'[8]

The *Joint Vision 2000* document, itself, was very explicit on the importance of space. The ultimate goal of United States military activities is called Full Spectrum Dominance, which is 'to defeat any adversary and control the situation across the full range of military operations,' which means United States forces must excel 'with access to and freedom to operate in all domains – *space*, sea, land, air, and information.'[9] (Emphasis added.) In its discussion of Precision Engagement, referring to space activities as well as all other operations, the document goes on to say: 'Precision Engagement is the ability of joint forces to locate, surveil, discern, and track objectives or targets; select, organize, and use the correct systems; generate desired effects; assess results; and re-engage with decisive speed and overwhelming operational tempo as required, *throughout the full range of military operations*.'[10] (Emphasis added.)

These official quotes should provide an understanding of how interested the Pentagon is in space warfare and anti-satellite capabilities. Soon there will be another report by a congressionally-mandated Commission to Assess United States National Security Space Management And Organisation which held its first meeting on 11 July 2000. This commission is mandated by the fiscal year 2000 National Defence Authorisation Act and is an extension of the Rumsfeld Commission – chaired by the new Defence Secretary Donald Rumsfeld and said to be composed of '13 distinguished private citizens.'[11] Those distinguished citizens consist of seven retired generals or admirals, three former Department of Defence officials, one former NASA official, one former House Armed Forces Committee member, and one senator. The word 'citizen' should not be confused with 'civilian.' The public will soon be hearing more platitudes on how important it is to 'defend' space.

Current anti-satellite activity

Anti-satellite development was slated to be cancelled entirely when President Clinton took office in 1993. But a small group of senators have been able to provide a tiny, unrequested amount of budget for ASAT each year. Since 1989 the Army has been quietly overseeing a joint-services Tactical Anti-Satellite Technologies programme featuring a hit-to-kill warhead, called the kinetic energy anti-satellite (KE-ASAT) weapon, similar to that being developed for ballistic missile defence.

1. Hit-To-Kill Warheads.

The kinetic energy anti-satellite programme began in 1989 as a means of leveraging off technologies developed for Star Wars. The 94-pound interceptor uses a visible light optical seeker to find and track the target while small computer-operated rocket motors guide the vehicle onto a collision course. It also has a shroud for the purpose of containing all the debris so as not to create space junk that would jeopardize United States spacecraft. All ground testing is completed for the kinetic energy anti-satellite weapon.

Although the Department of Defence has never requested funds for the kinetic energy anti-satellite weapon since at least 1995, Congress appropriated $30 million in fiscal year 1996 to perform hover tests. $50 million was provided by Congress in fiscal year 1997, and $37.5 million in fiscal year 1998. Boeing North America Inc's Rocketdyne Division (Canoga Park, California) is developing the system under contract to the United States Army. About $235 million had been spent on the kinetic energy anti-satellite weapon up to that point.

The kinetic energy anti-satellite weapon received no funding in fiscal year 1999 and the $7.5 million appropriated for KE-ASAT in fiscal year 2000 has not been released because no agreement has been released on a spending plan for the programme. According to Jack L. Brock Jr., Managing Director of Acquisition and Source Management for the General Accounting Office, 'Status of the KE-ASAT programme is currently in a state of disarray and [its] future remains uncertain.'[12] In 2000 the Department of Defence recommended that the Army complete existing programme contracts, place delivery of flight qualified vehicles in storage, and pursue no further development of the kinetic energy anti-satellite system.[13]

2. High Energy Lasers.

Destroying the function of a hostile satellite is preferable to smashing it to bits because it decreases the amount of space debris that United States satellites must encounter. For that reason, high energy lasers are a preferred anti-satellite weapon because they can blind spy satellites and burn out the electronics in others. High energy lasers may also be the only effective weapon against satellites in very high orbits.

A February 1996 Air Force report entitled *New World Vistas: Air and Space Power for the 21st Century* concluded: 'Control of space will become essential in the next decade ... [and] the United States may be called upon to protect non-military space assets from attack by terrorists or a rogue nation.'[14] The report recommended that the Air Force develop a ground-based high energy laser to destroy satellites. Besides the airborne laser and the space based laser, which are being developed as ballistic missile defence weapons, anti-satellite interests also centre on the Army's mid-infrared advanced chemical laser (MIRACL).

The mid-infrared advanced chemical laser was originally part of the Reagan Administration's Star Wars project but was cancelled by Congress in 1983. But Congress at the same time ordered MIRACL to be set up at the High Energy Laser Test Facility at White Sands Missile Range in New Mexico. There it has been used to support various Department of Defence tests since the late 1980s.

MIRACL is a megawatt-class deuterium-fluoride mid-infrared chemical laser which can hold a continuous beam on a target for up to 70 seconds. On 17 October 1997 – the same week that the White House used the line-item veto to kill the kinetic energy anti-satellite weapon – MIRACL fired two short bursts at an old United States Air Force satellite called MISTI-3. The test was reported to have successfully demonstrated the laser's ability to disable a satellite's spying capability. Senator Tom Harkin of Iowa described this as a test 'both unnecessary and provocative' which could induce other nations to build anti-satellite weapons.[15]

The Air Force also has the High Energy Research and Technology Facility in a remote area of the Monzano Mountains on Kirtland Air Force Base, New Mexico. This facility experiments in other directed energy weapons besides the killer laser. These include high-power microwaves, high-energy advanced pulsed power, and very-high-energy plasmas.

This Air Force laboratory has also come up with an 'all gas' chemical laser called all gas iodine laser (AGIL), which it claims would be ideal for use in space because of its light weight. It mixes nitrogen chloride and iodine gases in a vacuum to create the lasing action. Researchers believe it would take at least until 2003 to develop, demonstrate, and test the all gas iodine laser.

Conclusion

The hit-to-kill intercept tests that have taken place so far in ballistic missile defence programmes are really more representative of anti-satellite tests. The target comes from a known direction and a known speed at a known time.

Likewise, the high energy laser may be more effective against satellites than against missiles. With all the evidence and professional opinion opposed to ballistic missile defence – to say nothing of the political, diplomatic, and arms control nuances – one must wonder if there isn't an ulterior motive for such tenacity to missile defence activities. Ballistic missile defence programmes could well be a front for developing an anti-satellite capability. At the very least, a parallel effort. But, if so, why is anti-satellite development being done so clandestinely? Probably because the uproar of public opinion would be even greater and international dissent even stronger. Or maybe the capability needs secrecy to mask its first-strike connection.

During meetings in Geneva from late January until 18 February 2001, the United Nations Conference on Disarmament proposed that negotiations be commenced to establish new guidelines for banning offensive weapons in space and for limiting development of systems that could destroy spacecraft from earth. The United States blocked this proposal, saying there is no space race and that such a treaty is unnecessary. The United States further contended that the 1967 Open Skies Treaty and the 1972 Anti-Ballistic Missile Treaty are adequate in forbidding weapons of mass destruction in space. The United States has always maintained that its space efforts are purely defensive.

The flip side of the coin from learning how to destroy something is learning how to prevent it from being destroyed. One can pursue defensive technology and once the means of defence are known, the means of overcoming that defence can be developed. The United States Air Force has activated a Space Control Squadron at Peterson Air Force Base in Colorado. Its purpose is to study future concepts of offensive and defensive counter-space weapons. It may have been no accident that the United Nations proposal to establish new guidelines for space immediately followed the Pentagon's January 2001 exercise by the United States Air Force Space Warfare Centre at Shriever Air Force Base in Colorado, a war game which simulated a war in space in 2017.

The true natures of ballistic missile defence and anti-satellite capabilities are masked by the 'defensive' connotations under which they are presented to the public. It is hard to criticise anything that is truly defensive. There are two things wrong with this perception. First, it obviates any other means of settling international disputes which create the threat in the first place. Secondly, government and Pentagon reputation is replete with deception. What is presented to the public is not necessarily what is really taking place. In this case, the announced intentions do not reflect the capability the United States is seeking – a capability revealed by close study of how military development programmes fit together to achieve it. That is an aggressive first-strike capability which is neither defensive nor deterrent.

Whether there is skullduggery afoot or not, the technologies for ballistic missile defence and anti-satellite warfare are essentially one and the same. Both ballistic missile defence and anti-satellite warfare are critical elements of a first-strike capability. When combined with America's precision strategic missiles and anti-submarine capabilities, all interconnected and integrated through an intricate system of command, control, and communication, the first-strike capability is there. As all these technologies mature, that first-strike capability becomes more real. As the capability becomes more real, the more threatening it is to human values in all their nuances.

References

Aldridge, Robert C., *First Strike: The Pentagon's Strategy for Nuclear War*, (Boston, South End Press, 1983).

Cohen-2000 – *Annual Report to the President and the Congress*, by William S. Cohen, Secretary of Defence, 2000.

Defence News, (6883 Commercial Drive, Springfield, VA 22159-0500), various issues.

Department of Defence News Release 13July2000 – 'Commission On National Security Space Management And Organization Holds First Meeting,' released by Office of Assistant Secretary of Defence (Public Affairs), 13 July 2000.

Federation of American Scientists, Space Policy Project.

GAO-01-228R, *KE-ASAT Programme Status*, letter and briefing by Jack L. Brock Jr., Managing Director of Acquisition and Sourcing Management for the United States General Accounting Office, 5 December 2000.

Joint Vision 2000, released 30 May 2000.

Mercury News, (San Jose, California), various issues.

Newman, Richard J.; 'The New Space Race,' *U.S. News & World Report*, 8 November 1999.

Seeking A National Strategy: A Concert For Preserving Security And Promoting Freedom, the Phase II Report on a United States National Security Strategy for the 21st Century, by the United States Commission on National Security/21st Century, 15 April 2000.

SMDC Fact Sheet – 'Kinetic Energy ASAT,' a fact sheet prepared by the United States Army Space and Missile Defence Command, circa 1999.

SPACEDAILY: Your internet Space Portal.

Space News, 26 April 1993, p. 10.

Spohn, Lawrence; 'New 'All Gas' Chemical Laser Ideal For Space, Says Chemist,' *Scripps Howard News Service*, 11 August 2000.

STRATFOR – *'Race To Space,'* 27 February 2001.

SSG-IV – Premises For Policy: Maintaining Military Superiority In The 21st Century, 1999 Fiscal Report of Secretary of Defence Strategic Studies Group IV.

Vision For 2020, prepared by the United States Space Command, 2000.

Notes

1 Cohen-2000, p. 97.
2 *Space News*, 26 April 1993, p. 10.
3 For a more complete history of ASAT see Aldridge, *First Strike*, pp. 211-226.
4 *SPACEDAILY*, 10, June 2000.
5 Cohen-2000, p. 97.
6 SSG-IV, p. 17.
7 Seeking A National Strategy, p. 9.
8 *Vision For 2020*.
9 *Joint Vision 2000*, p. 8.
10 *Joint Vision 2000*, p. 28.
11 DoD News Release 13July2000.
12 GAO-01-228R.
13 GAO-01-228R.
14 Cited in *Defence News*, 26 February 1996, p. 4.
15 Cited in *Defence News*, 27 October 1997, p. 14.

Peace News

- ***the* international quarterly magazine for nonviolent activists**
- **published since 1936**
- **where nonviolent activists do their best thinking and reflecting**
- **for nonviolent revolution**

recent issues on: nonviolent interventions; Southern Africa; nonviolence and social empowerment; truth, forgiveness and reconciliation

current issue on economies of militarism
next issue on gender and militarism (out 1 June)

For monthly news by and for activists in Britain, buy *Nonviolent Action*

- ❏ Please send me a **free** sample issue
- ❏ I would like to subscribe. I enclose:
  - ❏ £10 standard   or   ❏ £20 supporting   **(UK rates)**
  - ❏ £15 joint sub to *Peace News* and *Nonviolent Action* **(UK subscribers only)**
  - ❏ £15 standard   or   ❏ £25 supporting   **(overseas rates)**
  - ❏ £_____ donation

TOTAL PAYMENT: £_____
Credit/debit card no. ____/____/____/____ **exp** __/__
Cheques £ sterling payable to "Peace News"
GIRO transfer to WRI giro account no. 585 20 4004 in Britain.
Name...
Address... SPOKES
Country...
Return this form to: *Peace News*, 5 Caledonian Road, London N1 9DY, Britain.
(+44 20 7278 3344; fax 7278 0444; email peacenews@gn.apc.org; www.gn.apc.org/peacenews)

subscribe today!

Scapegoats and Feral Cats

John Kinsella

John Kinsella teaches at Churchill College, Cambridge. He is joint editor of the literary quarterly Stand.

Working on the wheatbins at Mingenew, in the northern wheatbelt of Western Australia, in the early 80s, I witnessed the systematic slaughter of feral cats by high-powered guns. At an age where I'd grown out of the need to prove my passionate interaction with nature through 'the hunt', I found my sanity gradually decaying as my colleagues – aged nineteen through to their mid-twenties, spent their evenings down at the local tip, shooting feral cats and their offspring. At first I went along to be part vicariously of a social happening, an institutionalised element of a rural coming of age. But growing increasingly appalled by the slaughter, I retreated into myself and began the evolution towards a decision that would leave me vegan for life. In the red light of an 'outback' sunset, I still see D. jumping up and down on an old car bonnet, driving the cats out into the open, and 'blowing them away' with his pump-action shotgun. I see my co-sampler with his high-powered rifle, picking others off as they broke away. These people were military in their operation. It made for good stories at the pub, and was met with approval from all there. Cats were vermin and deserved shooting. Furthermore, they deserved to suffer. Half dead, swung around by their tails and flung into the rubbish piles. Kittens massacred by 12-gauge shot. Descriptions of dismemberment accompanied beers. I had to get out.

As a child I'd help set traps to catch 'the tiger', the biggest feral cat in the district. Something just too big to be left alone. A chook killer, a house-cat killer. And those native animals it predated on. Not to mention the rabbits, which weren't such a loss and were regular gun-fodder anyway – or so we said. Seeing that creature stiff and dead with its front paw chewed off in the frozen dawn was an earlier step in my evolution towards disgust. At the same time the crops were being planted, and the kangaroos further out being shot. People were clearing bush, and the salt was rising.

Native species were vanishing rapidly – because of the cats and foxes and other introduced predators, we were told, and reasoned. To kill a cat or a fox was to save the environment. I saw a documentary recently where blokes in an outback town allowed themselves to be filmed shooting cats. The documentary maker got off on the combination of blood lust and environmentalism. Here boys could be boys and do the right thing. Gender is an interesting factor here. The documentary maker was a woman who seemed to be getting some kind of sexual thrill out of the whole thing, while retaining an ironic distance. I've seen it many times. The boys being boys and the girls getting a bit messy and having a shot. No gender revolution there though, just patriarchy giving a little taste, under 'controlled' circumstances, bonding the woman to the bloke through a blood pact in which the bloke is the lead hunter. Rather like an initiation into a fraternity, with the cat as an enemy that needs to be eradicated. A neutral focus for blood lust, or for blood and lust. Drunkenness and sex follow. In Bridgetown I once heard two German girls say how they don't have room for this in Germany anymore, but 'down here you can get blood on you and have sex without complications'. Work that one out. It's a horror film.

The killing of feral cats is condoned by most who love nature. Leading environmentalists will turn from animal lovers to animal haters on this issue. Cats are evil. If we don't remove the feral cat from native Australian bushland, they'll say, there'll be no native species left. It doesn't belong, it has destroyed the balance. As have land clearing, the car, mining companies, other introduced species, spray, and so on. The problem is human – especially the use of European farming methods, intensive agriculture, the culture of profit. Removing the cat won't stop the disappearance of native species, it will just delay things. The cat is a scapegoat. The subtext of non-indigeneity is placed under pressure in a landscape devastated by colonisation. Selective indigeneity – remove lands from the original inhabitants, but be selective regarding which species can colonise. There's a racist subtext at work here. The cat becomes equated with unwanted migrant populations, and jokes about non-Anglo cultures eating cats abound. The cat symbolises the persistent vileness of the white Australia policy – it is the enemy of 'homogeneous' Anglo-Celtic Australia. There's more at stake here than simply ridding Australia of an unwanted killer of native species.

Some of the most vehement conversations I've had with fellow Australians have been over the feral cat 'situation'. Recently I had such a conversation with an eminent zoologist, a scientist I greatly respect, in a car driving out to Yorkrakine Rock in the central wheatbelt of Western Australia. The zoologist was talking about the crimes of the cat, and pointing out how whole populations of small native animals had been wiped out in her areas of study. These zones had been entirely changed by the presence of the cat and the fox. A whole new spatiality had to be developed to take their impact into consideration. She believed they should be ruthlessly and systematically eradicated. I can say quite honestly that her angle was a genuine one. There was no subtext at work that I could detect, just a genuine concern for the wellbeing of increasingly rare and endangered native species. In the same conversation she lamented that in her early writings she had not been more sensitive to the needs and concerns of Aborigines, that their environments had been destroyed in the same way – both by 'settlers' and by the animals they introduced. She created a moral and ethical connection. I pointed out the removing the cat did not correct the crimes of the state, and that the crimes would persist. The removal of cats is not land rights. But her point was a sincere one. She asked my opinion.

The feral cat, I said, is a scapegoat. It has been used to carry the sins of the invaders. In a sense, it's a weapon in the transformation of a space into something suitable for occupation. It has been used to erase identity. That's on the philosophical level. In reality it symbolises the inability of the invader to control his/her environment, to consolidate the conquest effectively. Out of control, it shows the destruction such 'settlement' has brought to the land. It is a symbol of failure. To appease the conscience, this stain on the hand must be removed – but no amount of 'out, out' will eradicate the crime because the destruction is all around us. And when that spot is gone the other spots will shine all the more obviously. The road at this point has been widened. Genetically modified crops are being tested. The delicate native ecosystem is being undermined in yet more deceptive ways.

As a vegan I don't believe in the killing or use of any animals. Obviously, if my child were at risk I would defend it, so there are extreme circumstances where I could see myself potentially 'hurting' something. But I avoid placing those I love in such situations. I feel we should behave responsibly in nature. I would not shoot a cat these days, and haven't since my teenage years when, quite frankly, I didn't know better and had read *Lord of the Flies* too many times and watched too many war films. I would not poison a cat. I don't condone others doing it. Why? The death of any creature is equivalent to the death of another. A life for a life doesn't add up for me. And fundamentally, because it doesn't stop the problem. Returning land to bushland, cessation of the farming of hooved animals which chop and destroy the topsoil, the end to chemical abuse, the abandonment of genetic modification, the winding down of polluting industries – these are all part of what's necessary. Do those things and get back to me. Otherwise, it's not even worth broaching as a subject. It's just not enough in itself. It is an excuse.

And so my argument went. My zoologist friend thought this over-the-top, illogical, impractical, and unsustainable. I pointed out that my rhetoric was intended to highlight inconsistencies in the anti-cat position. Of course it is deplorable to see native species demolished, to let the cat roam and destroy, but let's look at the cause as well as the effect. The imbalance is created in a variety of ways, not just one. We agreed to differ and went on to talk about saving sections of the forest by buying up those small bits still in private hands and setting them aside for posterity – a life's savings, spent saving a few hectares. A start. I admire her efforts greatly.

The story doesn't finish there though. There's a sting in this tale of feral cats.

I haven't been able to speak openly about this till now, for reasons that will become clear. When we arrived at a farm belonging to the zoologist's brother, we broke off in various directions and explored the area surrounding the house and sheds. I went straight for the rubbish tip, with its old sunshine harvesters and corrupted disk ploughs. These are the new wildlife zones – among the middens the spiders and snakes and insects create new territories. Then I heard the sound of feral kittens – suddenly, the spitting and hissing I know so well from childhood out on my uncle's farm, the sound coming from deep under the tank-stand, or in the old shed. Careful not to draw the attention of the others, I traced the sound to a large eucalypt hollowed at the base. Two kittens – scrawny, crazy-haired, were fighting. I crouched. In the half-light I could see the litter. They quietened down. The eyes shone. I moved away. I mentioned it to a fellow poet who'd accompanied us, knowing I could trust him not to mention it. 'If they find out, these kittens will be killed.' Driving home, I wanted to mention the beauty of these animals, of the situation – of the spatiality and environment of the rubbish heap – but kept quiet. The zoologist would have felt an obligation to the native wildlife to contact her brother. He would have found them in minutes – farmers know about things like this! So I avoided the scenario, the battle of consciences. I even avoided finishing a poem about it later in case the cats were still there. Months have passed and the kittens will have developed into fully-grown 'killing machines'. They are relatively safe now.

I pray for the native animals. I am on their side as well. But this is the order of things there now, and these cats have probably had a presence for dozens and dozens of generations. They are almost part of the place. Subtexts here too. That doesn't mean the territory shouldn't be reclaimed. But to kill the cats and leave the farm would be hypocritical – one brings the other. They are part of the same destructive machine. We should think about what it is we are worried about. What it is we have unleashed.

One of the most distressing aspects of the feral cat situation is the vanity of domestic cat owners. The desire to fetishise their animals, to own a pet as part of their home entertainment system. Cats are abandoned regularly, and it's not unusual for the very people who spend their time shooting cats to keep a pet cat at home. Such hypocrisy speaks for itself. A bell on the collar of a pet cat can save many native birds in the back garden. People keeping cats on the outskirts of the city, where the cats make regular forays into the fragments of remaining bushland, compound the problem. There's a lot to be said for common sense in this. The nature of the cat is not a sin in itself. Its very efficiency at hunting is its downfall. I find it disturbing to see so-called nature shows showing the big cats – the lion, tiger, leopard, panther, puma, lynx and so on – hunting and predating, as no more than sideshows for people's suppressed or not-so-suppressed bloodlust. People admire the exotic killer, yet condemn the ordinary feral cat. The answer to the 'problem' is not as simple as 'eradication'. For something closer to the truth we should look much closer to home – that is, within ourselves.

Stop the Ilisu Dam

Martin Hall

On 16th January 2001, the President of the World Archaeological Congress, Professor Martin Hall of the University of Cape Town, wrote to Prime Minister Blair to protest about British support for the proposed construction of the Ilisu dam in South East Turkey.

Dear Prime Minister,

I am writing to you in my capacity as president of the World Archaeological Congress in order to express grave concern with respect to your Government's proposed support for the construction of the Ilisu dam in South East Turkey.

As you will be aware, this particular project has been the subject of widespread criticism from many quarters. I am writing today with reference to fundamental issues concerning the human rights of the large and overwhelmingly Kurdish populations scheduled to be moved from their homes and resettled in advance of the flooding of towns and villages – specifically their rights with regard to the potential cultural heritage impact of the proposed dam.

The World Archaeological Congress (WAC) is an international forum for the discussion of all aspects of the past that holds large international conferences every four years attended by hundreds of archaeologists and other interested parties. Its continuing membership comprises concerned individuals from all five continents, represented between the four yearly meetings by regional representatives drawn from twenty-eight countries around the world. WAC has a particular interest in the areas of the protection, conservation and exploitation of the archaeological heritage, with a specific emphasis being placed upon the effect of archaeological and heritage work on the wider community and the responsibilities of archaeologists with regard to the cultural rights of indigenous peoples and ethnic minorities. To that end, an indigenous constituency is represented on the WAC executive.

World Archaeological Congress is aware that the Secretary of State for Trade and Industry, Stephen Byers M.P., has made it a condition for the granting of an export credit guarantee to the British construction firm Balfour Beatty that the Turkish authorities concerned, 'produce a detailed plan to preserve as much of the archaeological heritage of Hasankeyf as possible'. At present, a few archaeologists are struggling to document just a fraction of the archaeological material now under threat in that town. The World Archaeological Congress also notes with particular alarm press reports of last minute 'salvage archaeology' recently carried out at sites such as the Roman city of Zeugma/Apamea within the catchment area of the Birecik dam on the Euphrates River, another construction project under the management of the Turkish State Hydraulic Works. Such working conditions can never lend themselves to the fulfilment of the condition set with respect to the archaeological heritage at Hasankeyf.

In fact, the World Archaeological Congress believes that it would be very difficult to draw up and implement a satisfactory preservation plan in the circumstances prevailing in the region at present. In this regard, Congress would wish to make it clear to your Government that the cultural heritage impact of the dam reservoir extends far beyond the purely physical confines of Hasankeyf itself in two related ways.

Firstly, hundreds of different cultural sites, dating to every period of human history, fall within the total catchment area of the proposed dam reservoir, and are therefore threatened with destruction through inundation, or associated construction and irrigation works. Individual sites of local, regional and international significance include examples dating to the Neolithic, Chalcolithic, Neo-Assyrian, Late Roman, Byzantine and later medieval periods respectively. Many other sites of crucial importance to any adequate understanding of the more recent histories of the local populations in this region, including ancestral graveyards, are also under threat of destruction and/or prevention of access.

Secondly, from an archaeological perspective it is vital to consider the relationship between the physical archaeological material and the affected communities living in the area today. There are a variety of claims to aspects of cultural heritage made by differing sectors of the population located right across the catchment area of the proposed dam, of which the importance of Hasankeyf itself to Kurdish people is only the best known. These claims and different valuations of the past, whether disputed or not, must be outlined, researched and addressed in full, and those affected must be consulted and equitably involved in any decisions regarding further investigation of this heritage. This applies to Hasankeyf but also to all of the other archaeological material mentioned above. To date, there seems to have been inadequate consultation with affected communities in the area regarding cultural heritage and no serious attempt to involve them on an equal basis. Even less recognition has been given to their capacities and knowledge with regard to this impact or their rights to retain access to and use of cultural property.

In particular, the World Archaeological Congress must express grave concern that the vast majority of sites dating from medieval and modern times and of most direct relevance to the recent history of indigenous populations are in danger of being ignored altogether. The archaeology of these more recent periods has suffered most from the enforced brevity of archaeological surveys carried out thus far and archaeologists in the area are currently without the knowledge necessary even to begin to attempt adequate documentation. Such an oversight is all too readily made in the case of 'salvage archaeology' of the kind proposed for Ilisu, and can lead to the total submergence of the unrecorded material heritage of marginalised people.

The severing of people from the materials through which they understand their past has demonstrable traumatic effects, particularly when those people are already excluded, exploited or discriminated against. Several national and international bodies now emphasise the need for consultation with all sectors of project-affected communities on their cultural and social rights, the requirement to seek avoidance of detrimental impacts on those rights and in particular, the principle of free, prior and informed consent with regard to indigenous and tribal peoples. Like many other organisations, the World Archaeological Congress is currently considering the report of the World Commission on Dams, which was the most recent statement on such issues in the context of dams and which summarises the international rights framework for foregrounding the social, cultural and environmental impacts in decisions on building a dam or opting for an alternative. Congress also notes the emphasis on social inclusion and cultural diversity in the English Heritage review of policies relating to the historic environment – factors surely as relevant in South East Turkey given the nature of society in the region. Congress itself strongly supports the rights and capacities of indigenous peoples in the use and disposition of their cultural property including access to their religious and cultural sites (whether legally held or not) and recognises the rights of different ethnic groups to give consent over any proposed treatment of their dead. The code of ethics of the World Archaeological Congress includes an obligation 'to establish equitable partnerships and relationships between Members and indigenous peoples whose cultural heritage is being investigated' and 'to seek, wherever possible, representation of indigenous peoples in agencies funding or authorising research to be certain their view is considered as critically important in setting research standards, questions, priorities and goals'.

You will see immediately how cultural rights, as an aspect of human rights, are a key priority in archaeological work since obligations include responsibilities to those communities with whom archaeologists work. In relation to the Ilisu dam, the issues of cultural rights of affected communities, of the much broader range of archaeological material at risk and of the obligations of archaeologists in these two related instances, do not currently form any substantial part of your own Government's express condition with respect to the archaeological heritage of the region.

Adequate opportunities to discharge these professional obligations or to give voice to cultural rights are unlikely to occur at Ilisu, given the realities of the current political situation in South East Turkey. The prevailing circumstances of emergency rule in force in the region make it impossible to document the true extent of the cultural impacts of the dam in any archaeological preservation plan. It is not difficult to outline a likely scenario under the present circumstances, however. The World Archaeological Congress believes that the inadequate respect for human rights in this area, which includes violation of cultural rights, makes it very likely that those impacts will be severe, irreversible and disastrous for long-term social stability within affected communities and in the region generally. Congress considers that violation of social and cultural rights of affected communities, in the context of the lack of any attempt to avoid present and future impacts by seriously considering alternatives to the project, is legitimate ground for not proceeding with construction of the Ilisu dam itself.

The World Archaeological Congress asks that current and potential violations of this sort be regarded as the fundamental archaeological ground for reconsidering the United Kingdom Government's proposed funding of this project and, on that basis, requests that your Government withdraw its support for it immediately.

I thank you for your attention and look forward to your response.

Yours sincerely,
Martin Hall
President
World Archaeological Congress

Keynes: Man of Peace

Michael Barratt Brown

Michael Barratt Brown reviews Robert Skidelsky's John Maynard Keynes: Fighting for Britain 1937-1946 *(Macmillan, 2000).*

> 'But if nations can learn to provide themselves with full employment by their domestic policy... there need be no important economic forces calculated to set the interests of one country against that of its neighbours'
> J. M. Keynes, General Theory of Employment, Interest and Money, p.382

This is the third volume (another 580 pages) of Skidelsky's magisterial biography of Keynes. It is a worthy successor. It repeats the lucidity of exposition of complex economic ideas and the intimate interweaving of Keynes's personal and political lives. It is the story of a man confined to his bed from coronary disease at the start of this period of his life and for many days and even weeks of the remaining ten years. Yet during that period he crossed the Atlantic to the United States and back on ten occasions to engage as the leader of the British team in negotiations which lasted for weeks and sometimes months and on issues of the greatest technical complexity and political importance. Keynes was a big man and often appeared to his colleagues as somewhat larger than life. In this volume his wife Lydia Lopokova is given her rightful place as his constant companion wherever he went, his protector and nurse, sharing his impish love of life and art and human variety.

In the first two volumes Keynes was seen developing, from his First World War and post-war experience in government and from his teaching and management of finance at Kings College, Cambridge, the ideas which were to constitute the Keynesian revolution in economics. In this volume he is having to apply them to the real world. The passage quoted above taken from the last page of his *General Theory* provides the central motif that guided Keynes through the maze of conflicting interests from which the political and economic settlement emerged after the Second World War.

At the back of his mind, through all his economic argument and persuasive rhetoric, lay the firm conviction that there must not be a repetition after the Second World War of the inflation and unemployment in Britain and in Germany, and in the USA too, and throughout the world, that followed after the First World War. Every proposal that he made and every argument he considered had in the end to be judged by that one criterion. It was this that made it possible for him to cut through all the confusions and selfish interests that surrounded him.

None of this is to deny Skidelsky's central theme, that Keynes was 'fighting for Britain'. The military struggle was not his concern and after the Russians and then the Americans entered the war in 1941, the result was certain however long delayed. Keynes was concerned about winning the peace. The destruction that Britain suffered in the first years of the war and the expenditures incurred meant that Britain and the Empire could never again rival the power of the United States. But some means had to be found which would enable British finance and British industry to ensure full employment and a decent living for the British people after the war. As well as creating appropriate domestic policies, an international structure had to be established which would bind the wealth of the United States into maintaining full employment world-wide, or at least in Europe. It reads strangely today that 'full employment' appears so high among the aims of the Bretton Woods agreements. The avoidance of unemployment is said to be a matter 'not of domestic concern alone, but a necessary condition for the expansion of international trade.' It is put that way round.

How to pay for the war

Keynes's first concern on emerging from his sick bed early in 1939 was how the war could be paid for. His fear was that the overwhelming demand for resources for the war effort combined with full employment and the cutting off of civilian supplies from overseas would soon lead to a build up of demand far beyond what could be met. Inflation would be inevitable, with the poor suffering the worst, unless goods were rationed and expenditure controlled. Keynes did not like this alternative, although when the submarine blockade tightened, he recognised that it had to be accepted. He sought for a 'Middle Way' and believed that he had found it in a scheme of compulsory saving. Along with their income tax demands, income tax payers would be levied a proportion of their incomes and receive 'post-war credit' notes, to be cashed only when national resources allowed. Keynes's book *How to Pay for the War* appeared in February 1940 and Kingsley Wood's budget a year later introduced an element of compulsory saving to cover 3% of expenditure. Keynes had proposed 15%.

The scheme was vehemently denounced by the trade unions and most of the Labour Party. I recall desperately trying to defend it at a meeting in 1940 with the Communists in the Oxford University Labour Club. It raised two issues of very contemporary interest. The first is that Keynes had required the Treasury to prepare national income and expenditure accounts and estimates for the coming year to reveal the scale of the borrowing gap. He believed that this should not be greater than what could be regarded as capital investment. Gordon Brown is today following that advice. The second matter of interest is that of finding a scheme for deferred earnings in a period of full employment which could reasonably be regarded as acceptable by the workers. All attempts at incomes policies in Britain have failed because they applied only to wages and with no controls built in for the unions to exercise. Skidelsky quotes Richard Kahn saying that this was the 'stupidity of the leaders of the [British] trade unions', but where these policies have had more success in Scandinavia, profits as well as wages have been included and the unions involved.

In defence of Keynes's scheme, it has to be said that income tax, and the element of compulsory saving, was at that time progressively higher for higher incomes. The policy of subsequent Conservative Governments of increasing sales taxes would have been strongly opposed by Keynes as wholly regressive, bearing as they do most heavily on the poor. In the event prices rose between 1939 and 1945 by about 50%, most of this occurring before 1941. This is to be compared with the doubling of prices in the First World War, but there cannot be much doubt that this was more the result of rationing and price controls than of the compulsory savings. It was anyway a long time after the war was over that I opened a little envelope marked DO NOT LOSE and cashed what seemed to be a remarkably small sum of savings. I was not impressed and I am sure that others were not.

It is often averred that Keynes was insufficiently aware of the danger of inflation in his proposals for government spending to offset a failure in aggregate demand and neglectful of the importance of manipulating interest rates. The scheme for compulsory saving shows that he was very well aware of the inflation danger, though he did not believe, as some of his monetarist opponents do, that government spending is the sole source of inflation. He was certainly an enthusiastic advocate of cheap money and looked forward to the euthanasia of the *rentier* in the not-too-distant future, as human needs became increasingly satisfied. He would have been appalled at current levels of greed, although it is hard to know how his enjoyment of the life and appurtenances of a Sussex country gentleman could have been universalised. He would certainly have approved of a Tobin tax on speculation, which he himself indulged in but disapproved of as a way of conducting an economy. What would have depressed him most, had he lived to see it, was the absence of any justice in the development of the international economy.

The post-war international settlement
Keynes knew that post-war full employment could not be achieved by domestic policies only. There had to be an international framework within which these could succeed without the beggar-my-neighbour machinations of the inter-war years. Deficit countries (on their foreign payments) should never be forced to deflate their economies (by reducing demand for employment). Keynes did not believe in a protectionist self-sufficiency, although he sometimes glorified the

pleasures of what was home grown – as the modern protectionists like to quote him. He was a free trader, but within rules of the game that were 'fair' – a very English concept that has been adopted by the modern Fair Trade movement. He divided possible British policies in relation to American hegemony into three types: first, Austerity or 'Starvation Corner'; second, Temptation or giving in to American demands in order to get a big loan; and, third, Justice or Aid for Britain's and others' sacrifices while the United States had stood aside.

Skidelsky draws out very clearly from Keynes's many speeches, statements and cables that the American connection had in his view to be preserved. There was no future for the British people, Keynes believed quite passionately, in what he dubbed a Schactian policy. This was the policy of austerity and self-sufficiency plus bilateral trade agreements which Hitler's Finance Minister Hjalmar Schacht had applied to Germany in the 1930s. Britain's imports and exports had different origins and destinations. Britain needed a multilateral trade system and worldwide scope for its financial expertise. The possibility of a European Union, possibly to include even the Soviet Union, did not attract Keynes. He saw this as a continuation of the planned trade of the war years, which had its wartime justification but would prove to be a straitjacket in peace time. In this respect, Keynes was at odds with the majority in the unions and in the Labour Party.

To achieve justice the Americans had to be brought within a system that ensured that British purchases from the USA were paid for by the US, and that allowed Britain thereafter to balance her foreign trade without continuing to run a large dollar deficit. This was seen as a matter of justice, which he and nearly all the British public believed to be due to Britain and the empire after standing alone, running down their reserves, selling off assets to the Americans and in Britain's case running up vast debts to Sterling Area members. By the summer of 1941 the system of Lend-lease had been established for Britain's imports of war materials from the USA, but there were large debts left over from the previous two years. When the war ended with Germany Lend-lease would end, although it might be continued in part while the war with Japan continued. After that Britain must be free to re-establish export markets to pay her way. United States policy, however, was to force Britain to give up its imperial preference system and to free the sterling balances, so that Empire and Sterling Area members would all become free to buy American goods and invite American investment

Keynes's first proposal was for a Clearing Union which would allow free trade within the limits of each country's balances of exports and imports, and freedom of capital movements, but each country would be granted an overdraft facility as in a bank. This would not be accounted in national currencies but in a new international currency later called *bancor*. The United States would be bound to become the largest creditor and the object of the exercise would be to persuade the Americans to spend their surplus balances. To make the Union work like a bank, each member would deposit a required amount of its currency. The United States would be the largest depositor. The whole scheme would depend upon the size of the United States deposit and on the preparedness of the United States to wipe out the debts owed to it mainly by Britain. There wasn't a hope in hell that the Americans would fall for such a plan, but it forced them to produce something as an alternative, which emerged as a stabilisation fund and later a Monetary Fund and World Bank

What came out from the vast exchange of papers throughout the 1942 and 1943 discussions and the meetings at Atlantic City in 1944, which all led up to the agreement at Bretton Woods, was a very different animal than the one Keynes had thought up. The American alternative was largely the product of the brain of Harry Dexter White, who was later revealed to have been a Soviet agent passing back to Moscow all that was going on and having no desire to see a successful international order uniting British with American capital. In that respect he differed little from his American colleagues who hated and feared the Soviet Union; and Skidelsky argues that, while his actions were a betrayal of trust, White would not have thought that he was betraying his country. White's Stabilisation Fund and Reconstruction Bank were a part of his 'Grand Design', just as Keynes's Clearing Union, Relief Organisation, buffer stocks scheme and supra-national police force were part of his 'New Order'; and Skidelsky makes the point that White's Soviet sympathies would explain a desire to strengthen the Soviet Union at British and American expense.

The fundamental difference between Keynes's proposals and those that were agreed at Bretton Woods was the replacement of Keynes's semi-automatic banking system, supervised by international civil servants owing no national loyalties, by White's Fund and so-called Bank whose payments were managed and policed by boards of US appointed officials. It was even to be sited in Washington near to the seat of the US Government and not in New York near to the world's financial centre. Worst still, the resources at the disposal of the two institutions were agreed at $3.5 billion instead of Keynes's $25 billion. In place of Keynes's buffer stocks plan, which would have stabilised producers' incomes as well as prices, an International Trade Organisation was proposed to encourage trade exchanges. This was never ratified and in the end was replaced by the General Agreement on Tariffs and Trade, which simply agreed tariff reductions. Without any protection for commodity producers, mainly in the colonial territories, their prices and incomes were bound to collapse after the initial post-war shortages had been made good. Had the Keynes plan ever been accepted the disasters that have faced Third World countries over the last two decades could have been averted.

Keynes was fighting a hopeless battle. How hopeless it was becomes abundantly clear from Skidelsky's story of the negotiations that led up to the United States loan made to Britain in 1945. Keynes's battle with the Americans had always been about money. The Americans would give just enough to keep Britain afloat, but not enough to make her strong again. Keynes could call up all the rhetorical powers at his disposal and win the consciences and hearts of his ministerial adversaries one day, but the very next day their advisers and lawyers would return with documents that in no way reflected verbal understandings. Keynes would explode at 'a great nation being treated as if it were a bankrupt company', but that is just how the Americans saw Britain. The loan – a smaller sum in the end and with higher interest payments than had at one point been agreed – illustrates Keynes's dilemma. If he would not have Britain go it alone in austerity without the US, and he could not get payment in justice for Britain's war-time contribution, then he had to accept the 'temptation' of a loan. He had no fallback position and failed even to get the amount he wanted ($5 billion; he got $3.5 billion) and interest free or with waivers (the rate was 2% for 50 years with the possibility of deferments). For this the Americans on their side got agreement to the ending of imperial preference and the freeing of the sterling balances. Within a few months the sterling debts were being paid, exports were growing, but not fast enough to pay for the backlog, and the loan was exhausted.

It is not too much to say that the loan negotiations killed Keynes. He survived to defend the agreement in the House of Lords and to make one last journey to America to agree the final details of the Bretton Woods twins – the International Monetary Fund and World Bank. Keynes tried to reduce the political control of the US and failed. His comment afterwards was that 'I went to Savannah to meet the world and all I met was a tyrant'. During the train journey to Washington on the morning of March 19, 1946 Keynes collapsed. He and Lydia managed to return home, but within a month he was dead. Skidelsky writes very warmly of the man with whom he has been living as a biographer all these years. But he is less than euphoric about the contribution of the 'Keynesian revolution' to the post-war recovery in Europe. Here I think he is wrong, and I have the authority of the Clare Group of economists writing in the National Institute *Economic Review*, who see the post-war commitment of governments to full employment as critical. Skidelsky argues correctly that nationalisation and increased social services were not part of Keynes's scheme for slump control, nor American expenditure on armaments. The fact is that governments felt free to spend in circumstances where pre-Keynes they would have cut back.

As for the international framework, Keynes was largely defeated. There is no doubt that his defence of his proposals was heroic and brilliant, but Skidelsky doubts whether it made any difference. The Americans had in the end to come up with the sort of money Keynes was looking for – in the Marshall Plan. But by that time Britain and the empire had been downgraded. The loan was running out and the Sterling Area was fading. The rhetoric gave Britain a special relationship with the United States. In the reality of needing a bulwark against the Soviet Union, the Americans felt able to sponsor a European Union with Britain safely inside it, as a stalking horse if required. Keynes was always anxious to keep the Soviet Union within the comity of nations, he was opposed to the division of Germany and never seems to have used the anti-Soviet card in negotiating with the Americans. That is perhaps why his personal relations with Harry White seem mainly to have been happy. But, it cannot be denied that it was the existence of the Soviet Union and fear of Soviet power that encouraged governments to follow Keynes's ideas for ensuring full employment and expanding international trade.

As a tail-piece I should record the fact that Roy Harrod, Keynes's devoted follower and biographer, was active during the 1960s in the promotion of a Britain-Commonwealth-European Free Trade Association having some links of planned trade with the Soviet Union as an alternative to the European Common Market. As I sat on a committee with Harrod in this promotion, I asked him one day whether Keynes would have supported us. He said that he believed that he would and reminded me of one of Keynes's favourite put-downs: 'When circumstances change I change my mind. What do you do?'

Keynes was not opposed to planning, but it should involve as many participants as possible. What he hated about capitalism was the system of *laissez faire*, not the system of private property and enterprise.

THE ESSENTIAL E. P. THOMPSON

The most comprehensive collection of historical writings from the author of *The Making Of The English Working Class*.

508 pages   0 85036 505 8   £15.95

WORKING CLASSES, GLOBAL REALITIES

SOCIALIST REGISTER 2001

Twenty essays - an unrivalled range of thematic and regional themes.

403 pages   0 85036 490 6   £16.95

MERLIN PRESS, P O BOX 30705, LONDON WC2E 8QD.
orders@merlinpress.co.uk   fax +44 [0] 20 7497 0309   VISA MASTERCARD OR £ CHEQUES

POSTAGE: IN THE UK £1.00 PER BOOK

OUTSIDE UK £2.00 PER BOOK

THE BERTRAND RUSSELL PEACE FOUNDATION
PEACE DOSSIER

FULL SPECTRUM DOMINANCE

'Full Spectrum Dominance' is the key term in Joint Vision 2020, the blueprint the United States Department of Defence will follow in the future, from which these extracts are taken.

'The ultimate goal of our military force is to accomplish the objectives directed by the National Command Authorities. For the joint force of the future, this goal will be achieved through full spectrum dominance – the ability of US forces, operating unilaterally or in combination with multinational and interagency partners, to defeat any adversary and control any situation across the full range of military operations.

The full range of operations includes maintaining a posture of strategic deterrence. It includes theater engagement and presence activities. It includes conflict involving employment of strategic forces and weapons of mass destruction, major theater wars, regional conflicts, and smaller-scale contingencies. It also includes those ambiguous situations residing between peace and war, such as peacekeeping and peace enforcement operations, as well as non-combat humanitarian relief operations and support to domestic authorities.

The label full spectrum dominance implies that US forces are able to conduct prompt, sustained, and synchronized operations with combinations of forces tailored to specific situations and with access to and freedom to operate in all domains – space, sea, land, air, and information. Additionally, given the global nature of our interests and obligations, the United States must maintain its overseas presence forces and the ability to rapidly project power worldwide in order to achieve full spectrum dominance.

Achieving full spectrum dominance means the joint force will fulfill its primary purpose – victory in war, as well as achieving success across the full range of operations, but it does not mean that we will win without cost or difficulty. Conflict results in casualties despite our best efforts to minimize them, and will continue to do so when the force has achieved full spectrum dominance. Additionally, friction is inherent in military operations. The joint force of 2020 will seek to create a "frictional imbalance" in its favor by using the capabilities envisioned in this document, but the fundamental sources of friction cannot be eliminated. We will win – but we should not expect war in the future to be either easy or bloodless.

> **Source of Friction**
> - Effects of danger and exertion
> - Existence of uncertainty and chance
> - Unpredictabile actions of other actors
> - Frailties of machines and information
> - Humans

The requirement for global operations, the ability to counter adversaries who possess weapons of mass destruction, and the need to shape ambiguous situations at the low end of the range of operations will present special challenges en route to achieving full spectrum dominance. Therefore, the process of creating the joint force of the future must be flexible – to react to changes in the strategic environment and the adaptations of potential enemies, to take advantage of new technologies, and to account for variations in the pace of change. The source of that flexibility is the synergy of the core competencies of the individual Services, integrated into the joint team. These challenges will require a Total Force composed of well-educated, motivated, and competent people who can adapt to the many demands of future joint missions. The transformation of the joint force to reach full spectrum dominance rests upon information superiority as a key enabler and our capacity for innovation.'

SON OF STAR WARS

This letter was published in The Times in March 2001 to coincide with the visit to Washington of British Defence Minister Geoff Hoon.

'During his visit to Camp David last month, Prime Minister Blair appears to have reached an accommodation with President Bush on the contentious issue of missile defence, saying that he understood and shared the US concern about the threat from weapons of mass destruction and would work closely with the US to consider the options and implications.

It is almost a year since the five largest nuclear powers gave a clear written undertaking 'to accomplish the total elimination of their nuclear arsenals leading to nuclear disarmament' and the world awaits an indication of how this objective is to be achieved. Many agree that the implications of missile defence include destabilising international relations, undermining existing arms control treaties and causing a new nuclear arms race. Some of the options being considered under the umbrella title of missile defence would require the use and further development of the Fylingdales radar station and Menwith Hill communications centre, both in North Yorkshire.

Defence Minister Geoff Hoon will be meeting his US counterpart Donald

Rumsfeld in Washington on 19th March for talks on key issues, including missile defence. He stated recently that: 'As its closest ally, we would, of course, want to respond helpfully should a request [to use any facilities in Britain] be made by the United States' (*Hansard* 12th February). This rather sounds like a diplomatic 'yes' to a proposal that hardly upholds the stable strategic relationships that the Prime Minister values.

We find it unacceptable to be told repeatedly that the government has no opinion on missile defence. This, for example from Foreign Office Minister Keith Vaz: 'No specific proposal is on the table but when such a proposal is available for discussion, it will be discussed in the proper way' (*Hansard* 27th February).

May we suggest that 'the proper way' is to consult the British public and debate it in Parliament.'

This letter was signed by
Malcolm Harper, Director, United Nations Association
Dave Knight, Chair, Campaign for Nuclear Disarmament
Peter Nicholls, Chair, Abolition 2000 UK
Dan Plesch, Director, British American Security Information Council
Gill Reeve, Assistant Director, Medact

NUCLEAR WEAPONS, UNCERTAINTY AND THE LAW

There is good reason to believe that any threat or use of a 100 kiloton UK Trident warhead would be open to serious legal doubts. The Government responds by stating that 'the United Kingdom's minimum nuclear deterrent is entirely consistent with international law'. However, we need more information before we can assess the validity of this claim. Answers to several questions are required, as the World Court Project (www.gn.apc.org/wcp) spells out.

The Government case
If challenged about the legality of Trident, the Government uses the following arguments:
- The 1996 Advisory Opinion of the International Court of Justice (ICJ) did not rule that the threat or use of nuclear weapons would be illegal.
- The legality of the potential use of nuclear weapons is to be determined by the criteria which apply to any form of weapon.
- The determining factor is the specific circumstances in which they are to be used.
- Hypothetical speculation about such circumstances serves no useful benefit.

These arguments were developed in the written and oral submissions made by the United Kingdom and United States to the International Court of Justice in

1994 and 1995 when it was considering requests by the World Health Organisation (WHO) and the UN General Assembly (UNGA) for Advisory Opinions on the legal status of the threat of use or nuclear weapons.

Nuclear Weapons in General?

The arguments in the submissions all refer to nuclear weapons generally, and never to specific types. This is not surprising, as the requests for Advisory Opinions were couched in general terms. Letters to the Government about Trident are therefore usually met with replies about nuclear weapons in general. However, if, as is generally accepted, nuclear weapons are subject to the same legal restraints as any form of weapon, then discussion in the United Kingdom must revolve around Trident, the only nuclear weapon system it deploys.

Hypothetical situations

In spite of the Government's reluctance to entertain hypotheses, the International Court of Justice submissions contain references to possible legal use. Speaking for the United Kingdom in November 1995, Attorney General Sir Nicholas Lyell said, 'Let me take an example. A State or group of States is faced with invasion by overwhelming enemy forces. That State or that group of States is certainly entitled to defend itself. If all the other means at their disposal are insufficient, then how can it be said that the use of a nuclear weapon must be disproportionate?' The US oral statement referred to situations 'such as a small number of accurate attacks by low-yield weapons against an equally small number of military targets in non-urban areas'. The United Kingdom written statement on the World Health Organisation request claimed that 'modern nuclear weapons are capable of precise targeting, and many are designed for use against military objectives of quite small size'. The emphasis is on limited use of low-yield weapons.

On 15th November 2000, during the Lord Advocate's Reference proceedings arising out of the Greenock case, Duncan Menzies QC, Advocate Depute for the Crown, provided an interesting example of the possible legal use of UK Trident.

'...if the nuclear power aggressor was threatening the territorial integrity of a non-nuclear victim state, let's take it, the example of China being a nuclear power threatening New Zealand, a non-nuclear power, with a battle fleet armed with nuclear missiles which it was stating it was about to fire at New Zealand and which battle fleet was in the Pacific, approaching the point at which the state of New Zealand was in range of its nuclear missiles, in such a situation I submit that it would be consistent with international law, including humanitarian laws applicable to armed conflict, for another nuclear power to use nuclear force against that battle fleet...'

Already, questions arise:

1) **Why was the United Kingdom Trident system, with its 100 kiloton warheads, not referred to in the United Kingdom submissions to the International Court of Justice?**

2) Would the Ministry of Defence endorse the example provided by Duncan Menzies QC of how Trident might be used lawfully?

Doubts about Certainty

The United States and United Kingdom submissions consistently presuppose that those arguing for illegality claim that all nuclear weapons have certain 'inherent' characteristics which inevitably make their threat or use incompatible with international humanitarian law. Thus the United Kingdom written statement on the World Health Organisation request refers to 'those who maintain that *any* resort to nuclear weapons by a state which is attacked will *inevitably* lead to an escalation in the conflict...' and 'It has sometimes been argued that the use of nuclear weapons would inevitably violate this principle' [Unnecessary Suffering]. In referring to the principle that civilian populations must not be made the object of attack, the United Kingdom claims that 'the essence of this argument is that nuclear weapons cannot be used in a way which enables a distinction to be drawn between combatants on the one hand and civilians and civilian objects on the other. They are thus said to be *inherently* indiscriminate weapons'. [emphases added]

These are not isolated examples: the submissions are full of such language.

We can accept that nothing can be predicted with certainty. However, a successful challenge to the United Kingdom Government's position would not have to show that any threat or use would be inherently illegal under any circumstances. It would only need to show the improbability of lawful threat or use in any plausible scenario. Although nuclear weapons are subject only to the same legal restraints as any other weapon, the International Court of Justice stated that because of the 'unique characteristics of nuclear weapons... the use of such weapons in fact seems scarcely reconcilable with respect for [the principles and rules of law applicable in armed conflict]'. If this is true of nuclear weapons in general, it must apply all the more forcefully to a 100 kiloton Trident warhead.

Risk assessment

From publicly available documents and correspondence with the Government, we still have little idea of how it estimates risk. Risk assessment means estimating the probability of a decision having an unintended but pernicious outcome, and multiplying it by the seriousness of that outcome. A small risk of a disaster would weigh more heavily than a moderate risk of a minor problem. With just one 100 kiloton Trident warhead, let alone the current load of three in each United Kingdom missile, the outcome could be catastrophic.

The International Court of Justice recognised that 'The destructive power of nuclear weapons cannot be contained in either space or time. They have the potential to destroy all civilisation and the entire ecosystem of the planet'. However small the probability of such an outcome on a particular occasion, the enormity of a potential catastrophe produces a result beyond the limits of human calculation.

What is at issue here is the risk of contravening international humanitarian law. In her Dissenting Opinion, Judge Higgins pointed out: 'there has been considerable debate, as yet unresolved, as to whether this principle [that civilians may not be the target of attack] refers to weapons which, because of the way they are commonly used, strike civilians and combatants indiscriminately, or whether it refers to whether a weapon, 'having regard to (its) effects in time and space' can 'be employed with sufficient or with predictable accuracy against the chosen target" Her first alternative would tend to outlaw nuclear weapons in general. Her second one requires examination of particular nuclear weapon systems.

To be convincing, the United Kingdom Government must therefore argue that the risk of law-breaking arising from the threat or use of Trident is almost zero. It must be shown that any use of Trident would carry virtually no risk of nuclear escalation, serious damage to neutral states, or disproportionate civilian casualties. There must be practically no question of missing the target due to variations in the weather, microscopic blemishes on the delivery vehicle or minor faults in the guidance system.

We must also bear in mind that our experience of nuclear detonations on civilian populations is limited. There have only been two (Hiroshima and Nagasaki), in both of which the destructive power was less than a fifth of a Trident warhead.

The same approach applies to any possibility that a Trident missile might be launched by accident or miscalculation. It is not sufficient to claim that such a possibility is very remote. It must be shown to be effectively excluded over the whole lifetime of the system. We must be convinced that there is no room for human error. Unless this is true, the deployment of Trident amounts to recklessness.

The next questions are therefore:

3) **Without a serious and publicly available probability analysis of the potential results of a Trident strike, how can the Government assure us that no threat or use of Trident could risk violating the law?**
4) **Is the Government confident that Trident could be used with sufficient or predictable accuracy against the chosen target?**

Balancing the Consequences

Sir Nicholas Lyell told the International Court of Justice that 'even a military target must not be attacked if to do so would cause collateral civilian casualties or damage to civilian property which is excessive in relation to the concrete and direct military advantage anticipated from the attack – an aspect of the wider principle of proportionality to which I have already referred', but that 'this rule requires a balance to be struck between the concrete and direct military advantage anticipated and the level of collateral civilian casualties and damage foreseen' and 'the greater the military advantage which can reasonably be expected to result from the use of a weapon in a particular case, the greater the risk of collateral civilian casualties which may have to be regarded as within the law'.

Clearly a balance between military advantage and collateral damage is envisaged. This is the crux. We accept that, in the nature of things, no future scenario can be foreseen precisely. However, we have been assured that 'legal advice would also be available to Ministers if circumstances were extreme enough for us ever to have to consider the use of nuclear weapons to defend ourselves from the attack. We are satisfied that our arrangements to ensure informed legal advice in such circumstances are fully adequate...' and 'legal advice from the Government's legal advisers was available to Ministers and senior officers and officials in considering the Strategic Defence Review' [Douglas Henderson, Minister of State for the Armed Forces, letter to Nigel Waterson MP, in response to a letter from Leslie Dalton, 1 June 1999].

Legal advice in a nuclear emergency would not spring from a vacuum. We can assume that criteria (as opposed to 'hypothetical speculation') do exist for balancing military advantage with collateral civilian casualties in the event of a nuclear strike. We need to know more about these criteria. Simply to say that legality depends on the balance between military advantage and civilian suffering is not enough. There is the problem of comparing different orders of criteria. The military advantage of destroying a particular target can, in principle, be assessed. In a utilitarian world we can, with great difficulty, imagine how values could be attached to the lives and wellbeing of a specified number of civilians. What seems incomprehensible is how anyone could make the comparison between the value of a very large number of lives and a specific military advantage. We therefore need to understand the United Kingdom Government's procedures and principles for making these assessments. These basic criteria can hardly qualify as state secrets. We therefore need to know:

5) **What are the general criteria for determining the balance between military necessity and suffering to civilians arising from the use of Trident?**
6) **What are the general theoretical sources of these criteria?**
7) **Is the Government confident that, even if these criteria were well understood by lawyers and decision makers well beforehand, they could be relied upon to provide secure practical, moral and legal guidance during a nuclear emergency?**

Effects on people

These criteria must surely include the effect of a 100 kiloton Trident warhead on any civilian population living at or near likely nuclear targets. On 10 January, 2000, Jeremy Corbyn MP raised this issue in a question to the Secretary of State for Defence. The answer yielded the information that computer modelling had taken place 'which enables us to assess the effects of nuclear detonations'. The factors taken into account included 'the yield and design of the weapon used; the accuracy of the delivery system employed; the nature and construction of the target; the characteristics of the surrounding terrain; the height of the detonation; and geological and weather conditions'. The factors listed do not include the crucial one – the likely effects on the civilian population. Without this, neither the public at large nor the lawyers advising the government can make an informed legal assessment. So we have another question:

8) **Has any assessment been carried out by the United Kingdom Government of the effects of a 100 kiloton Trident warhead detonation on a civilian population living near a nuclear target? If so, is there any good reason why the results should not be made public?**

Nuclear secrecy

A Ministry of Defence letter has stated: 'nor does the Government believe that any conceptual planning on potential use of nuclear weapons carried out by the Ministry of Defence can reasonably be made open to public scrutiny. Secrecy in this area plays an important part in enabling the United Kingdom to maintain a credible minimum deterrent capability at the lowest possible level'. [Stephen Willmer to Angie Zelter, 2 March, 2000]. It is one thing to invoke the need for secrecy in matters of military capabilities and planning. It is quite another to claim it for the legal thinking governing these vital issues. This should be open to democratic accountability. So we need to know:

9) **Why does the Government decline to disclose the legal criteria governing the possible use of Trident?**
10) **If these criteria are treated as secret, how can the courts operate effectively in cases involving citizen disarmament of Trident?**
11) **How can ordinary citizens, who honestly doubt the legality of the threat or use of Trident, hope to act with probity without access to the Government's legal criteria?**

Reprisals

One aspect of the legal criteria for the threat or use of Trident gives rise to special cause for concern. The United States stated orally to the International Court of Justice that 'the customary law of reprisal permits a belligerent to respond to another party's violation of the law of armed conflict by itself resorting to what otherwise would be unlawful conduct'. The US written statement referred to Additional Protocol 1 to the 1949 Geneva Conventions which contains prohibitions on reprisals against civilian populations. 'These are among the new rules established by the Protocol that... do not apply to nuclear weapons'. This view was echoed in the United Kingdom oral statement. It is to be hoped that this interpretation does not imply a view that a nuclear reprisal directed towards the civilian population as such could ever be lawful.

12) **Can the Government confirm that under no circumstances would Trident ever be even threatened, let alone used, against a civilian population as such?**

Legal scrutiny of trident needed

The very least that can be concluded from this assessment is that the legality of

Britain's nuclear policy is open to question. However, on 23 August 1999, George Robertson, then Secretary of State for Defence, wrote to Austin Mitchell MP, 'Thank you for your letter of 22 July 1999 requesting a meeting to discuss the legality of Trident. I am afraid that such a meeting would serve little purpose. We have repeatedly made our position clear. We do not consider the possession or use of nuclear weapons as such to be illegal'. The delegation would have consisted of three MPs and Lord Murray, a former Lord Advocate of Scotland. They had asked for discussion about UK Trident in particular, not nuclear weapons *as such*. There was a complete refusal to discuss the matter, even with very well-informed and distinguished people, and with no real reason given – merely an unsupported assertion. This is only one of several examples of attempts to raise the issue which have been rejected without proper explanation – which is why we need to ask one more question;

13) Will the Government recognise that the legality of the threat or use of Trident is open to serious doubt and therefore deserves the fullest public scrutiny?

HIROSHIMA CONFERENCE

The 2001 World Conference against Atomic and Hydrogen Bombs will take place from August 3rd to 9th in Hiroshima and Nagasaki. Its theme is 'Nuclear Weapons States Must Make Good on Their Promise to Abolish Nuclear Weapons'.

More than sixty million people in Japan have signed the 'Appeal from Hiroshima and Nagasaki' for the elimination of nuclear weapons. The signature campaign has spread to many parts of the world. However, the leaders of the United States and other nuclear weapons states will not voluntarily eliminate their nuclear weapons. Despite the official promise to 'eliminate their nuclear arsenals,' the United States Government continues its Missile 'Defence' Plan, fuelling the nuclear arms race, and its tests and development of nuclear weapons. The Japanese Government, despite being the only country to have suffered attacks with atomic bombs, and having a peaceful constitution, supports United States nuclear weapons, saying that Japan is under the US nuclear 'umbrella.' The Japanese Government concluded secret agreements with the United States to bring nuclear weapons into Japan and make Japan a foothold for a nuclear war, which would be initiated by the United States. An increasing number of United States warships call at Japanese civilian ports. Frequent ultra-low flight training and night-landing practice and the planned construction of a new base in Okinawa inflict serious damage on the people, and are met with growing opposition and protests by citizens and local councils.

The Organising Committee of the World Conference against A & H Bombs has called for common actions across the world in support of the abolition of nuclear weapons. They can be contacted by e-mail (antiatom@twics.com).

STOP BOMBING VIEQUES!

In April 2001, the Governor of New York, Republican George Pataki, is visiting Puerto Rico. He will see for himself the situation on the island of Vieques, where more than 9,000 people live. The US Navy has used Viecques for military exercises and as a bombing range for more than 60 years. Depleted uranium munitions are thought to have been fired there.

Governor Pataki stated that 'we are happy with the President's suspension of bombing in March, but we want the immediate and permanent cessation of bombing, not in three years; we want the Navy to leave Vieques now.'

The announcement of the visit by New York's Governor is in response to the unanimous approval by the Puerto Rico State Legislature on the 26th of March of a resolution calling for the 'immediate and permanent cessation of all activity by the US military on the Island of Vieques.'

Nilda Medina, spokeswoman for the Committee for the Rescue and Development of Vieques, commented that 'the visit by Pataki adds to a list of other prominent figures in public life who support the movement to get the Navy out of Vieques.' She added that Pataki's visit takes on extra importance since he is a powerful member of the Republican Party and is close to President George Bush.

The Committee for the Rescue and Development of Vieques can be contacted at P.O. Box 1424 Vieques, Puerto Rico 00765, Tel. (787) 741-0716 e-mail:bieke@coqui.net

ASLEF

General Secretary: **M.D. Rix**. Assistant General Secretary: **M.F. Blackburn**
9 Arkwright Road, Hampstead, London NW3 6AB
Telephone: 020-7317-8600 Fax: 020-7794-6406
Email: Info@ASLEF.ORG.UK   www.aslef.org.uk

Fraternal Greetings to all your Readers and Supporters

World Peace Remains our Goal

The Campaign to Scrap Nuclear Weapons Must Continue

We Must Oppose Bush's Star Wars Programme

Reviews

Branding

Naomi Klein, *No Logo*, Flamingo, 490 pp., £8.99

This is a brilliant book about brands – Adidas, Barbie, Body Shop, Calvin Klein, Coca Cola, Disney, Gap, Heineken, Levi, Marlboro, McDonalds, Microsoft, Nike, Pepsi, Reebok, Shell, Starbucks, Virgin, Wal-Mart and many more. It's about how they get us to buy! buy! buy! theirs and only theirs. And how they respond to our resistance. But it's also a book about the sweatshops and destruction of communities and the environment where many of the goods are made. The story that Naomi Klein has to tell is one for the most part of avarice, insensitivity and ruthlessness that makes the exploitation of Victorian employers seem like compassion. But the message is that we are playing the game of the brand makers and if we wish to, we can stop them. More than that, she shows that here and there we are stopping them.

It's an interesting word – branding. It originally meant marking by burning with a hot iron, like the Nike swoosh tattooed on the sportsman's back. It's a mark that is supposed to last. So the brand is not just a product you buy, but becomes part of you; branding is an entry into a new way of life; your shoes and clothes, furnishings and cars give you self-esteem; what you drink reaches to all parts of you. The logo ceases to be just a label, it is a cultural icon. You're not cool unless you have the right gear. So gym shoes and sneakers become trainers. Pizzas and burgers are not a food but an experience. Drinks are not for your thirst but for your ego and your virility. The new car will get you the beautiful girl. Disney's cartoons turn into Disneyland. Shops are restyled as branded villages. And so it goes on. Perhaps it's not all bad. Anita Roddick, founder of the Body Shop, is quoted saying that her 'stores are not about what they sell, they are the conveyors of a grand idea – a political philosophy about women, the environment and ethical business.'

So, it's dangerous territory this; such claims like all the others can easily be ridiculed. People are not all so gullible. Catch them young is the admen's watchword, and Naomi Klein shows example after example of advertising and promotion in schools, of campus agreements on food and drink tenders, on computer installation and above all on sports sponsorship. Everywhere there is the influence of TV, and in 273.5 million households worldwide, we are told, that TV is MTV watched by 85% of US teenagers – 'an all-news bulletin for creating brand images'. Much of the attraction is in the folk heroes who show off the new gear. Famous athletes are paid vast sums to appear in the latest shoes or sports kit, thousands of times more than the women making the goods. When ridicule and opposition get too strong, the brand response is to accept the criticism and turn it round, as in jujitsu. It's cool to wear your jeans torn and faded; ok, we'll make them like that. They want diversity; we'll give it them. 'You can beat a brand to death' some critics say. So they extend the product range and the reach.

The political as political

Naomi Klein is engagingly self-critical about her years as a feminist against porn, as a champion of blacks and defender of gays and lesbians, fighting for their recognition on the campus, in the work place, in the media, when all the time, she says, 'the 'personal as political' had come to replace the economic as political and, in the end, the political as political as well.' What she realised in the 1990s was that the admen found her and her friends interesting. The search for identity among the excluded in the 'identity politics' of the time could be worked on for street styles, edgy music, colourful pix in the ads, and for exploiting a new way out of social exclusion. A market for diversity could be widened from the white middle classes to poor blacks and Latinos in the US and out beyond that to Asia and Africa and the Americas.

The real tragedy opening out in front of the young Naomi Kleins was that everywhere in the world poor parents and whole families were scrimping and saving so that the kids could have the latest in T shirts, jeans and trainers and a Sony personal CD player. 'They prefer Coke to tea, Nikes to sandals, Chicken McNuggets to rice, credit cards to cash', as a senior US economist, Joseph Quinlan, was writing in the *Wall Street Journal* by 1997. The media grabbed stories of selling drugs, stealing and mugging to buy what came to be called 'disposable status wear', but, as Naomi Klein discovered, it was generally mother's minimum wage or welfare check that was going on buying the $150 Air Jordans.

Beneath this development of branding into new products and new regions, two further threats were emerging to weaken American society and by extension others too. The first was that the power of the big brand companies to influence educational institutions and even governments was growing. Grants of money from these companies for hard pressed universities, schools, colleges, even states had become of great importance. Any criticism of this role could endanger staff tenure. Teaching and research increasingly followed lines which would not offend the donors. This became all the more important as the second threat emerged. This was the threat to American jobs. To supply the new mass markets, and to maintain the mass advertising that they implied, production costs had to be held down. More and more of the actual production of branded goods was transferred to Asia and Latin America.

Cheap labour in the Third World could be combined with advanced machinery and computer controlled designs to undercut any producer in the United States. Even that was not enough. The young women employed had to work for long hours in appalling conditions as well as for starvation wages, and submit to sexual harassment, as the production processes were sub-contracted to local employers enriching themselves without local regulation. Export Processing Zones were promoted as steps towards the real economic development of poor countries. It hasn't happened. They didn't build factories there but only what a Philippine economist called 'labor warehouses'. And, if there was 'trouble', like swallows they flew away.

Sweatshop production in the mass markets for consumer goods began to be revealed early in the 1980s, but it took ten years for a movement of protest to grow worldwide to the point of the Seattle demonstration at the World Trade Organisation meeting in 1999. This mass gathering brought together student radicals rejecting their teachers, trade unions whose members had seen their jobs taken away, and concerned consumers wishing to be able to wear clothes and eat food that had not been produced under inhuman conditions. Seattle was the climax of what Steven Greenhouse in *The New York Times* in March, 1998 is quoted by Naomi Klein as calling 'the biggest surge in campus activism in nearly two decades'. 'At Duke, Georgetown, Wisconsin, North Carolina, Arizona, Michigan, Princeton, Stanford, Harvard, Brown, Cornell and University of California at Berkeley', she reports, 'there were conferences, teach-ins, protests and sit-ins – some lasting three or four days.'

The gathering wave of protest

Naomi Klein ends on an optimistic note as she acclaims the gathering wave of protest against sweatshop manufacturing. The protesting crowds in Prague, in Nice, at Davos and wherever the rich and powerful meet to decide our fate, suggest that her hope is not misplaced. Her chapter on 'Reclaiming the Streets', however, reveals that there is a mindless violence in some elements of these crowds that is understandable enough, but will hardly widen their support. The best hope lies in the opening up of connections worldwide through the internet. Naomi Klein quotes information about Nike flowing 'freely via e-mail between the US National Labor Committee and Campaign for Labor Rights; the Dutch-based Clean Clothes Campaign; the Australian Footwear Campaign; the Hong Kong-based Asian Monitoring and Resource Centre; the British Labour Behind the Label Coalition and Christian Aid; the French *Agir Ici* and *Artisans du Monde*; the German *Werkstatt Oekonomie*; the Belgian *Les Magasins du Monde*; the Canadian Maquila Solidarity Network – to name but a few of the players.'

There is still, however, a lack of an alternative on offer. What shoes and clothes and electronic equipment are *not* made with sweatshop labour? It would be good if the big brands would permit the workers who make their products to organise and thus to raise their wages and improve their conditions. But such a possibility seems remote. It would be good if some manufacturing industry was retained in the industrially developed countries, but such a possibility seems even more remote. The way forward through fair trade which has been pioneered with coffee and tea and chocolate is easier to establish with such primary commodities from the cooperatives of small-scale farmers than it is with goods from large scale manufacturing. But it is a way forward. As more consumers come to reject the output of the sweatshops as well as the products of plantation exploitation, the alternative will become more realisable. Producers and consumers will unite against their common enemy.

Michael Barratt Brown

The Last of Old Labour

Brian Brivati, *Guiding Light: The collected speeches of John Smith*, Politico's, 287 pp. £18.99

John Smith came into Parliament in June 1970, and made his maiden speech in

November. It was on family income, and made comparisons between the Speenhamland regime, and the Heath Government's policy on poor relief. The intervention was short, and to the point. As his editor says, it passed off 'successfully without making any discernible impact'.

Brivati has read through a million not dissimilar words in order to distil this book, and he succeeds in showing us a far more complex figure than that of mythology, which sees Smith only as 'a safe pair of hands', or a dependable right-winger.

Brivati succeeds in showing us a far more complex figure, committed to radical action in a number of fields. Although he was identified with the centre right, Smith had worked harmoniously with Tony Benn at the Department of Energy, and with Michael Foot at the Department of Employment. Foot had steered through the repeal of Edward Heath's legislation on industrial relations, so that Smith needed close and effective liaison with the trade unions. There does not appear to be any sign of friction during the course of this task. The centre right in the days before Tony Blair was sternly Old Labour. It understood the unions not only as power bases, but also with sympathy for their social objectives. Where it showed impatience this was frequently more to do with union conservatism than with any notion of trade union excess.

Brivati quotes an interview with David Frost on Clause IV:

'*David Frost* Clause 4 – going through the various areas where people want to know answers – Clause 4, are you going to repeal Clause 4?

John Smith Well I don't think that's the heart of the matter actually, I think the important thing is the practical policies which the Labour Party will bring forward. We are a party of the mixed economy, we've always been a party of the mixed economy …

David Frost Well why keep Clause 4?

John Smith Well I don't think there's any great point in arguing about theology, I'm fairly relaxed about that. What I'm concerned about is …

David Frost Don't tell me you're a local pastor, worrying about, talking about theology …

John Smith Well I'm using it strictly in the sense of party politics in the sense, but you're quite right in the sense, one shouldn't be disparaging about theology at all and let me take that back, I apologise to theologians everywhere. But I believe the number of tasks we've got to do; let me just give three areas of policy which I'm very committed to …

David Frost Yes alright, you do that … I think you're underestimating the degree to which, though Clause 4 may not be, may not be a dead letter in your mind but it's a litmus test for people out there. Do they mean what they're saying, do they mean to modernise – why are they keeping that? I think it's a litmus test.

John Smith Well I've never heard anybody on the doorsteps, certainly not a wavering voter saying to me 'what about Clause 4?' Have you tidied that up yet? … I don't really think that is where the matter …'

With hindsight, we can see that Clause IV, 'theological' or not, served as a ratchet on public policy. It was Clause IV which made it possible for Tony Benn to think about 'the fundamental and irreversible shift in the balance of income and power'. The removal of Clause IV said plainly that in the fields of public ownership, enterprise, and service, anything was reversible. Anything (everything?) goes. It was all up for sale.

For this reason, Smith's speeches, cautious and moderate though they undoubtedly are, are light years removed from the actions of the Blair Government.

Brivati thinks that

> 'He might not have liked elements of the style of this Government; he would not have bought into the importance attached to the packaging and he would have been less interested in the way New Labour sometimes follows fashions, especially in the media, but he would have approved of the substance, content and consistency of purpose that the Blair government has so far demonstrated on the issues which mattered most to him: education, employment, health and, yes, the creation of an optimistic democracy.'

But, an impartial reader of the gospel according to John Smith would think that this is all far too kind. Consider Smith's judgement of what he called 'The Thatcher experiment' ...

> 'Not only do we have the economic waste of unemployment, we have an industrial economy which is smaller, receives less investment, produces less output, and has the most adverse – and deteriorating – balance of trade in our modern economic history. Even worse ... the technological base of British industry is disturbingly weak. We simply are not developing the new products and processes which can alone pioneer new industries for the future...'

In every one of these areas, Blair has equalled and surpassed the achievements of the Thatcher experiment. What was Smith's remedy?

> 'I join battle with enthusiasm with those on the right who believe that the only way is through unrestricted market forces and that the role of the State is minor.'

That is why Smith gave us speeches on the theme 'The Market is not Enough'. Gordon Brown may well examine other of Smith's dicta with some interest:

> 'The constitutional position of the Bank of England in relation to the Government is satisfactory at the moment. I see no reason why that should be changed. A wide range of powers is available to the Chancellor of the Exchequer and no Chancellor should willingly give them up. He certainly should not contemplate handing over power over key economic monetary issues to bankers who are not accountable to the British people.'

Did then, Smith establish the lines subsequently followed by New Labour in its priority areas?

The Blair administration has not even marginally advanced the education or health services, spending less than the Major administration in its concluding years. But it has begun a plague of initiatives to privatise schools and hospitals, mortgaging the education and health services for years to come. Its employment policies have certainly been hyped to the high heavens, but they have been far removed from those of their predecessor. And the 'optimistic democracy' which we have evolved is about to reveal the highest rate of abstention/disgust seen in recent times.

Brivati thinks that the Blair administration has given Britain a stable economy: but Blair's continuation of the politics of Thatcherism have actually continued to undermine manufacturing, and to run up immense imbalances of trade and payments. Meantime, the rail system remains dangerous in the extreme, and has intermittently to close down altogether. The same dispensation is about to be extended to the London Underground. When the plague of foot and mouth hit British agriculture, the Ministry of Agriculture, Fisheries and Food, deployed almost half as many vets as its forerunner in 1967, at the time of the last epidemic. Those public services which could not be sold had commonly been closed.

No, if Smith today offers us any guiding light, it can help illuminate the values of the past. Any possibility of a different future will depend on whether his Party can recover from the invasion which has subdued it, or whether it can be reinvented.

Ken Coates

The Politics of Corruption

Robert Williams et al, Four volume set, *Edward Elgar***, 2448 pp. Hardback £530.00**

An extraordinarily broadly drawn collection of essays and analyses is combined in these four heavy volumes, to offer a remarkable overview of the politics of corruption, North and South, East and West. The interaction between private and corporate wealth, and the public power has always been prone to generate some tendencies to corruption. The evolution of neo-liberalism has opened a wide area of new possibilities in this field. Robert Williams and his colleagues have explored much of the literature of the last three decades, from a wide variety of academic disciplines.

Their four volumes are grouped as follows: the first, edited by Williams himself, seeks to provide an overview and explanation, featuring papers on the theory of corruption and its victims under different political systems. The second volume, under the aegis of Professor Williams and Professor Theobald, concentrates on the phenomenon of corruption in the developing world, and ranges over Latin America, Africa and Asia. There are two papers on corruption in the Peoples Republic of China, but otherwise the volume draws its evidence from former colonial territories.

A third volume, compiled with the help of Jonathan Moran and Rachel Flanary, covers corruption in the developed world, and the development of clientilism and organised crime. There are four chapters on different aspects of the problem in the United States, and twice as many on West European corruption. But corruption in Italy is the subject of four further papers, which are, perhaps misleadingly, separated from the area of Western Europe, and grouped under the heading of Southern Europe.

Britain provides a case study on the corruption of British politics and public service, and a further essay on lobbyists. There are three papers on Russian corruption, drawn from a rich field which might easily have generated a volume of its own.

The final volume, edited jointly with Professor Doig, concerns the remedies for corruption, from codes of conduct through to legal sanctions. The oldest study in the book dates from 1961, and concerns the theorism of the experience of corruption in former British West Africa. A number of other studies date only from 1999, so that these volumes contain a good deal of strictly contemporary material.

This is a timely collection, unfortunately: and there is a great deal of evidence that it will need to be updated from a rich seam of new materials, before very long.

Meantime, these volumes belong in every decent library of political science and economic development.

James Smith

$E=mc^2$

David Bodanis, *$E=mc^2$ A Biography of the World's Most Famous Equation*, Macmillan, 2000, 324pp, £14.99

David Bodanis's book gives a very readable and comprehensive background to the famous equation $E=mc^2$. At the same time, it provides an accessible account of radioactivity and radiation. The author explains how the universe is full of radiation, and also why the Earth should not be. Radioactivity occurs naturally. But, since 1945, the sometimes reckless contributions of human beings have led to radiation catastrophes. These include high level radiation incidents such as the A bombs and Chernobyl, but also the low level incidence of radiation such as that demonstrated by the radioactivity of post-1945 steel. The author also explains the dangers associated with uranium and plutonium, which is especially topical during the current scandal concerning depleted uranium.

Pamela White

The Great Sell-Out

Dexter Whitfield, *Public Services or Corporate Welfare*, Pluto Press, 2001, pp.314

Dexter Whitfield is the founder of the Centre for Public Services which has for 30 years been developing strategies for trade unions and local communities in the

UK and many other countries including Australia, New Zealand and the USA. On the basis of this wide experience he has now written what must become the basic text for all those concerned with the takeover by capital of the welfare state as we have seen this unfolding through the neo-liberal economic onslaught and the so-called Third Way reforms. The book provides detailed statistical and documentary evidence of the whole process of what Whitfield calls Corporate Welfare taking over from the universal provision of the Welfare State. If you want to find the facts of what has been going on, you will find them here, all carefully referenced and simply and easily explained for the general reader as well as for those more expert in this field.

This book is, however, more than a textbook of the current development of the welfare state. Its sub-title is *Rethinking the Nation State in the Global Economy*, and the study of the translation of welfare from the state to corporate control is set in a world-wide perspective. Whitfield is careful not to suggest that the state is disappearing under the onslaught of capital, but that it is being transformed in a new partnership of state and capital in which capital becomes increasingly the dominant partner. Collectivity is replaced by individual responsibility and welfare is narrowed down to benefits for the needy and excluded in place of universal public provision. Whitfield shows how great is the loss, but also what can still be done to save what has been built up in social solidarity over the years.

MBB

E. P. Thompson

Dorothy Thompson (Ed.), *The Essential E. P. Thompson***, Merlin, 498 pp. £15.95**

This anthology from the writings of Edward Thompson will whet the appetites of new students, and warm the hearts of many far older students (and agitators), who came under the great man's spell. Dorothy Thompson must have found it very difficult to make the choices embodied in this book: but it must be said that they are good choices, and they will rekindle our awareness of the breadth of Edward's vision, and the purity of his commitment.

Four extracts from *The Making of the English Working Class* start the book with a bang, and lead it on through a treatment of Mary Wollstonecraft to excerpts from William Morris. This section of the work is given the title 'Politics and Culture', and to emphasise this view, it concludes with an excerpt from Thompson's study of the relationship between Edward Thompson the elder, and Rabindranath Tagore. The second and third sections concern Law and Custom, and History and Theory. They are capped off by two items on the reading and writing of history.

Dorothy Thompson has done her husband proud, and this book will ensure that new generations of admirers will swell the ranks of the old.

KC